JUDAH SCEPTER

JUDAH SCEPTER

A HISTORICAL AND RELIGIOUS PERSPECTIVE

Brian Arundell Howard of Wardour

iUniverse, Inc.
New York   Bloomington

Judah Scepter
A Historical and Religious Perspective

iUniverse books may be ordered through booksellers or by contacting:

iUniverse
1663 Liberty Drive
Bloomington, IN 47403
www.iuniverse.com
1-800-Authors (1-800-288-4677)

Because of the dynamic nature of the Internet, any Web addresses or links contained in
this book may have changed since publication and may no longer be valid. The views
expressed in this work are solely those of the author and do not necessarily reflect the
views of the publisher, and the publisher hereby disclaims any responsibility for them.

ISBN: 978-1-4502-3976-9 (pbk)
ISBN: 978-1-4502-3978-3 (cloth)
ISBN: 978-1-4502-3977-6 (ebk)

Library of Congress Control Number: 2010908674

Printed in the United States of America

iUniverse rev. date: 6/16/2010

For
Michael, Sue, Mary, Father Barthel, Sister Elizabeth
Honor of
H.E. Thomas Arundell of Wardour
Recognition of
All Contributing Sources

Contents

CHRONOLOGY

	~3000 – 2600 BC	Building of Troy I
	~3000 – 2600 BC	Building of Troy II
	~2300 – 2000 BC	Building of Troy III
	~2300 – 2000 BC	Building of Troy IV
	~2300 – 2000 BC	Building of Troy V
Zarah (Zeus)	~1600 - 1500 BC	Beginning of Royal Lines
	~ 1500 BC	Dardanus journey to Troad
Laomedon has Troy built by Poseidon and Apollo	~1300 BC	Building of Troy VI
	~1300 BC	First establishment of oracle at Dodona
	~1200 BC	Building of Troy VII
	1191 BC	First Trojan War begins
	1181 BC	Fall of Troy
Death of Priam King of Troy	1181 BC	Helenus journey to Epirus
	1181 BC	Aeneas journey to coast of Italy
	~1180 BC	Oracle at Dodona
	~ 1149 BC	Second Trojan War
	1000 – 800 BC	Oracle of Apollo at Delphi
	677 BC	Third Trojan War
	677 BC	Trojan settlement in Black Sea Region
	550 BC	Croesus test of the seven Oracles, Delphi becomes supreme
	~480 BC	Oracle of Delphi prophesies the Persian invasion and their defeat at the Isle of Salamis

	~ 480 BC	Persian invasion of Greece
	445 BC	Trojan settlement in Pannonia
Antenor I King of Trojans	416 BC	Trojan settlement of Upper Rhine
	356 BC	Birth of Alexander the Great
	~ 332 BC	Alexander the Great conquest of Persia
Frankus King of the Franks	13 BC	Decree to name of Franks under rule of Frankus
	†	Jesus born and Resurrection
Marcomir IV	21	Ruling Line (Zarah) marries Priesthood line (Pharah)
	312	Oracles under Constantine considered a pagan religion and lessens influence
Constantine the Great	~ 330	Reformation of Roman Empire, Byzantine Empire, Constantinople
	361	Decline of the Oracle
	370 – 430	Beginning of Frankish opposition to Roman Empire
	450	Merovingian Dynasty
Clovis King of all the Franks	511	Christianity brought to the Franks
Queen Brunhilda	~ 575	Frankish Absolutism
	670	Mayor of the Palace established
Charles Martel	732	Battle of Tours
	~ 745	Carolingian Dynasty
Pepin	749	Franks Protectorate of the Papal State
	753	Meeting of Charles and Pope in the woods
	753	Charlemagne crowned King of the Franks
Charlemagne	801	Crowning by Pope as Holy Roman Emperor
Alfred the Great	849 – 899	
	1066	Battle of Hastings
Hereward	1070	Camp Refuge

	1099	The First Crusade
Fulk V King of Jerusalem	1131	
	1135	Plantagenet Era begins
William d' Albini I	1138	Creation of Earls of Arundell
	1147	The Second Crusade
Henry II King of England	1153	Rule over England and lands in France
Richard the Lionheart	1191	The Third Crusade
Edward I	1271	
	1337 – 1453	100 Years War
Robert Howard	1385 – 1436	Dukes of Norfolk new creation
	1455 – 1487	War of the Roses
John Howard, Duke of Norfolk	1485	Commander of Richard III army died in Battle of Bosworth Field ending War of the Roses
Sir Thomas Arundell		Knighted by Henry VII for valor in Battle of Bosworth Field
	1492	Christopher Columbus discovers America
Queen Katherine Howard	1540	
Charles Howard	1587	Spanish Armada
Saint Philip Howard	1557 – 1595	Elizabeth I discord with the Royal Court
Baron Thomas Arundell of Wardour	1595	Battle of the Gran, Rudolph II Holy Roman Emperor
	1607	Jamestown Settlement May 14
	1618 – 1648	30 Years War, Treaty of Westphalia
	1634	Journey to Maryland and Americas, Arc and the Dove
Thomas Arundell Howard	1653	Howard's Mount Granted

James II	1686	Recognition of Decree in letter to Thomas Howard
Clement Howard Sr. Brigadier General British Army	1754 – 1763	French and British War, Treaty of Paris
Clement Howard Jr. enlisted Revolutionary Army	1776	Declaration of Independence
	1804 – 1998	Dormancy of Holy Roman Empire, Imperial Title, Crown, Throne
	1999	Restoration of Holy Roman Empire, the Imperial Title, Crown, Throne

PREFACE

The guidance and direction of the populace throughout the Bible, as well as the Grecian era, the Roman era, and our own modern day has been, to a great extent, entrusted to the royal family of Judah [the lion] and their acceptance of a precedence over time. Judah Scepter carefully documents this truth in the form of history and religion. A refreshing perspective of history on a broad scale is presented about the royal family that migrated from one continent to the next while accepting the prevailing will of their time to guide the populace to a better life. An examination is made into the impact that royal family members have had on history with their struggles and actions to reign over the temporal world for the betterment of mortal life, while aspiring to become closer to the spiritual world with God.

The main thrust of Judah Scepter is that there is a continuance of ideas from one generation to the next by the royal family, while aspiring to the same qualities from the beginning of the royal family of Judah. The direction taken by these royal descendants was to increase and unite the populace in the areas of culture, territorial boundaries, faith, justice, and administration. Revelations will be presented throughout to help illuminate the world's history; Judah (Zeus) is the god depicted in literature and father of the royal family bloodline; the Trojans rebuilt their citadel in the Troad many times over, not just when defeated by Achilles; Charlemagne's descendants have three separate lineages in Britain; and Arundell Howard was part of the first successful colonization of America under Lord Baltimore. The royal family from Judah will be revealed and their actions and struggles examined.

Judah Scepter shows that the essence of the royal genealogical lineage never changed as they moved from one region to the next, just the name they used to signify who they were including Trojan, Frank, and Norman. Research has shown that the royal lineage was from these tribes. Later they adopted surnames usually taken from the area where they lived or composed by a popular idea or belief in such a way as the tribes developed from names Tros, Frankus, and Hereward. Their journeys have led them from one great city to the next including Dodona (Greece), Troy, Pannonia (Hungary),

Belgium, Paris, Aachen, Wessex, Anjou, Cornwall, Norfolk, and Baltimore. The task of including as many individuals as possible from the royal family of Judah in this text was managed by its scope and the historical impact of the individual. These individuals such as Helenus of Troy and Thomas Arundell Howard of England excel in the traits of virtue, piety, strength, courage, and faith.

Helenus was a Trojan, seer, captain, son of Priam, and so revered by the Trojan people that his name was used for thousands of years after his death. He fought on the main lines during the Trojan War against the Achaeans. Helenus was entrusted by his family members to instruct the Trojans on how to please the gods and foretell future events to win victory. During the fall of Troy, injured and turned away from the hand of Helen, he fled to the great Mount Ida. After surviving the carnage of Troy, Neoptolemus captured him and took him back to Epirus where he remained until he could finally return and liberate the city of Troy for his people.

Over three thousand years later Thomas Arundell Howard also sought to survive a war and bring his family to a land where they could live and prosper. Thomas, who was the son of Baron Thomas Arundell of Wardour, Count of the Holy Roman Empire, fled the civil war in England with his family to America, specifically the inlet shores of Maryland. The journey to get there was most risky and many hardships were to follow their arrival. The people who preceded the new immigrants did not fare well against the many diseases and other severe challenges that beset them. Coming from a military and Catholic family, Thomas mustered the strength to overcome these obstacles and founded both Howard's Mount and Pomfret Field in Maryland. These journeys, along with many other actions and struggles of the royal descendants will be scrutinized.

We also explore why, how, and to what advantage did the royal family of Judah adopt the three precedents. The precedence that changes through time is the Will of God – Will of Zeus – Justice, Christianity, and Duty and Faith. In the book "City of God" by St. Augustine it is presented to the reader how God is developing His chosen people as if they are His children. Thus, St. Augustine posits how God is creating a growth pattern for His chosen people in the way of laws and expectations of individuals. This book will parallel these attempts by the precedence accepted over time by individuals of the royal family of Judah. Thus as the journey proceeds the precedence of the time are adopted allowing them to both grow and strengthen the people.

The first precedence Will of God – Will of Zeus – Justice applies during biblical times and to the period after Jesus Christ around 200 AD. Through biblical text, historical text, and the thoughts of individuals of the time these were important factors in the lives of a given descent of people. As the royal lineage and people adopted these they also increased, flourished, and eventually created a new race of people. The people spoken of are the Hebrews, who became the mighty race of the Trojans of Troy whose father was Zarah (Zeus), the son of Judah (Zeus). Two great conflicts during this era were the Holy War of Amun and the Trojan War. Judah would find allies in the Mediterranean region to suppress the advances of the Egyptian army. Two cities would battle during this period, the Achaeans of Greece and the Trojans of the Troad. The Trojans united with its neighboring allies, and the Achaeans with all of the Greeks in the Mediterranean. Homer in the "Iliad" would recounts this historical war called the Trojan War in story form. The reasoning of St. Augustine in the "City of God" can be overlaid onto these two great conflicts. The Trojans took a separate path in their move to the Upper Rhine region while the Greeks battled with the Persian army for centuries.

> *"Our wills, therefore, exist as wills, and themselves whatever we do by willing, and which would not be done if we were unwilling. But when any one suffers anything, being unwilling, by the will of another, even in that case will retains its essential validity – we do not mean the will of the party who inflicts the suffering, for we resolve it into the power of God."*

Christianity was the second precedence accepted, during the time after Jesus Christ around 200 AD to the present time starting with the Franks. One must do three things to fully accept Christianity as an individual: accept the teachings of Jesus Christ fully and intellectually, be baptized, and spread Christianity to other people. As this was adopted, it increased the territory and unity of the people, which produced a structure for the future progress of the people. Two Great Kings, Constantine of the Roman Empire and Clovis of the Franks, would accept this faith and each would become its protectorate, a fourth and supreme form of acceptance. The Franks would develop a new empire under this religion, The Holy Roman Empire, with the aid of the Pope and the Papal States. This would be the first formal doctrine to initiate the divinity of God in both the spiritual and temporal realms. The Pope would administer the spiritual, to aid and protect the souls of men. The Holy Roman Emperor would administer the temporal, to aid and protect the mortals who currently live in the world created by God.

As there were kings, high officials, priests, and priestess (Oracles) in ancient times, a new form of organization would form. Kings, Dukes, Counts, and Barons under the Holy Roman Emperor and bishops, archbishops, and priests under the Pope became the new administration for the divine will. Both the temporal and spiritual would work in harmony with one another, one no higher than the other and each relying upon the other for the same divine reason. The reasoning of St. Augustine in the "City of God" can be overlaid onto this administration and summed up into one paragraph.

> *"For it is to God that sacrifices are offered at their tombs – the God who made them both men and martyrs, and associated them with holy angels in celestial honour; and the reason why we pay such honours to their memory is, that by so doing we may both give thanks to the true God for their victories, and, by recalling them afresh to remembrance, may stir ourselves up to imitate them by seeking to obtain like crowns and palms, calling to our help that same God on whom they called."*

When the age of the Franks ended, their descendants continued to advance the spread of Christianity. This was primarily accomplished through Crusades and the establishment of churches and monasteries. The Crusades were an important idea in the lives of many but none more than a family descended from Charlemagne who called themselves the Plantagenets. These Crusades were both successful and unsuccessful depending on one's viewpoint and which of the five crusades is being discussed. Christianity was widely accepted on the European Continent and practiced by the nobility up until the sixteenth century when it split apart. Royal families of the time had churches they were associated with and supported other countries abroad in this matter of spreading Christianity as did the Arundell, Howard and Plantagenet.

The last precedence, Duty and Faith, was applied during a time of extreme faith for the Holy Roman Empire, the Emperor, and determination to prosper in the new lands of America. Members of the royal family of Judah began to apply valor by looking beyond their own welfare to aid others in being able to practice their ideas and faith. These individuals of strength, virtue, and piety would gain great fortune and acclaim abroad. Their duty to others and mercy to their common enemies would be the great example for centuries to come. These men of duty and faith would hold the two great surnames in history, Arundell and Howard. The reasoning of St. Augustine in the "City of God" can be overlaid onto this principle of being royalty while at the same time practicing the ideas of duty and faith, summed up into one paragraph.

> *"This is the origin of domestic peace, or the well-ordered concord of those in the family who rule and those who obey. For they who care for the rest rule-the husband the wife, the parents the children, the masters the servants; and they who are cared for obey-the women their husbands, the children their parents, the servants their masters. But in the family of the just man who lives by faith and is as yet a pilgrim journeying on to the celestial city, even those who rule serve those whom they seem to command; for they rule not from a love of power, but from*

a sense of the duty they owe to others- not because they are proud of authority, but because they love mercy."

An undertaking of such a grand scale would seem almost unattainable without the aid of plentiful resources and time. The research for this book took several years in the areas of genealogy, history, religion, and biographies. The collected history and biographies were from organizations, state historical societies, libraries, family documents, and the Royal Historical Society. The main source of genealogy was the Bible, St. Augustine, Bartholome Gutierrez, Church of the Latter Day Saints, Maryland Public Offices and Private Sources. The work was done separately on each category until completed, and then brought together to produce the result.

The intent of this book is to spread the knowledge of both religion and history bound and defined by precedence in time upon a royal family of Judah. Thus, the aspiration is to show how the royal family journeyed over time doing the will of God and shaping who we are today. The understanding of how great together is the will of God and one's individual will is the main purpose of this text, for both were the creators of this divine journey. The genealogical chart shows the royal lineage that makes up Judah Scepter.

JACOB (KRONOS)
JUDAH (JUPITER)
ZARAH (ZEUS)
DARDANUS
ERICNTHONIUS
TROS
ILLUS
LAOMEDON
PRIAM
HELENUS
GENGER
FRANCO
ESDRON
GELIO
BASABILANO
PLESRON
ELIACOR
GABERIANO
PLASERIO II
ANTENOR I
PRIAM II
HELENUS II
PLBSRON
BASABILIANO II
ALEXANDER
PRIAM III
GETMALOR
ALMADION
DILUGLIC
HELENUS III
PLASERIO
DILUGLIO
MARCOMIR
PRIAM IV

HELENUS IV
ANTENOR I
MARCOMIR I
ANTENOR II
PRIAM V
HELENUS V
DLOCLES
BASSANUS
CLODOMIR I
NICANOR I
CLODIUS I
ANTENOR III
CLODOMIR II
MERODOCHUS
CASSANDER
ANTHARIUS
FRANKUS
CLODIUS II
MARCOMIR III
CLODOMIR III
ANTENOR IV
RATHERIUS
RICHEMER
ODOMIR
MARCOMIRIV
CLODOMIR IV
FARABERT
SUNNO
HILDERIC
BARTHERUS
CLODIUS III
MARCOMIR V
PHARAMOND
CLODIUS

MEROWIG	ADELBERT (SON)	
CHILDERIC I	WAMBERT	
CLOVIS	AUSBERT	
CLOTHAR I	ARNOALDUS	
SIGEBERT I	ST. ARNULF	
CHILDEBERT II	ANCHIUS	
THEUDEBERT II	PEPIN OF HERISTAL	
EMMA	CHARLES MARTEL	
EROCENBERT	PEPIN	
EGBERT	CHARLEMAGNE	
WIHTRED OISCINGA	PEPIN I	LOUIS I (SON)
AETHELBERT II	BERNARD	LOTHAR I
ALBURGA	PEPIN	ERMENGARDE
EGBERT III	HEBERT I	REGNIER I
ETHELWULF	HERBERT II	REGNIER II
ALFRED THE GREAT	ROBERT	REGNIER III
AETHELFLAED	ADELAIDE DEVERMANDOIS	LAMBERT I
AELFWYN	FULK III	LAMBERT II
ALWARA	ERMENGARDE DEANJOU	HENRY II
LEOFRIC III	FULK IV	GODFREY II
HEREWARD	FULK V	ADELIZA (MD.)
ROBERT HOWARD	GEOFFREY V	WILLIAM ALBINI I
JOHN HOWARD	HENRY II	WILLIAM ALBINI II
JOHN HOWARD	JOHN LACKLAND	RENFRED ARUNDELL RALPH ARUNDELL
WILLIAM HOWARD	HENRY III	RENFRED ARUNDELL
JOHN HOWARD	EDWARD I	JOHN ARUNDELL I
JOHN HOWARD	ALICE DEHALES	JOHN ARUNDELL II
JOHN HOWARD	MARGARET PLANTAGENET	JOHN ARUNDELL III
ROBERT HOWARD	JOHN MOWBRAY	JOHN ARUNDELL IV

JOHN HOWARD	THOMAS MOWBRAY	JOHN ARUNDELL V
ROBERT HOWARD (MD.)	MARGARET MOWBRAY	JOHN ARUNDELL VI
JOHN HOWARD		JOHN ARUNDELL VII
THOMAS HOWARD		THOMAS ARUNDELL
EDMUND HOWARD		JOHN ARUNDELL X
MARGARET HOWARD (MD.)		THOMAS ARUNDELL

	MATTHEW ARUNDELL	
	BARON THOMAS ARUNDELL	
	THOMAS HOWARD	
	WILLIAM "CAPTAIN" HOWARD	
	WILLIAM HOWARD	
	CLEMENT HOWARD SR	
	CLEMENT HOWARD JR. PHILIP HOWARD JORDAN HOWARD I JORDAN HOWARD II	

I

JACOB, JUDAH, ZARAH
THE SCEPTER
AND
LION

The scepter will not turn aside from Judah, neither the commander's staff between his feet, until Shiloh comes, and to him the obedience of peoples will belong.

Gen. 49:10

For Judah himself proved to be superior among his brothers, and the one leader was from him.

Chron. 1 5::2

THE SCEPTER LINEAGE BEGAN by the passing of God's will from one generation to the next starting with Jacob's blessing unto Judah. The designation of where the royal line was born is interpreted in biblical history and St. Augustine's "City of God". Upon examining these holy texts one will begin to see how the divine nature of things evolved through oracles, blessings, and birthright. God first shows His divine will through His oracle in a dream to Jacob, then by the blessing of Judah, and next through birthright to Zarah. Each in his own way earns this royal right of inheritance by doing the will of God and then by passing the will of God unto others. This divine journey thus begins with Jacob to do the will of his father and comes to a place where he finds there is a higher will of God. The path and will of God now begins and, as will be shown, many journeys follow by the royal descendants, each with their own duty to perform but with the same will.

Jacob was the younger of two sons, Esau being his elder brother, who made a bargain and agreement between each over primacy. Esau the elder immoderately lusted over things while the younger Jacob prepared food for his father and was a simple man "without guile". When Jacob's father Isaac grew old his eyesight began to fail and when he went to bless the elder he instead blessed the younger who put himself under his fathers' hand. The blessing is:

> *"See, he says, the smell of my son is as the smell of a full field which the Lord hath blessed: therefore God give thee of the dew of heaven, and of the fruitfulness of the earth, and plenty of corn and wine: let nations serve thee, and princes adore thee: and be lord of thy brethren, and let thy farther sons adore thee: cursed be he that curseth thee, and blessed be he that blesseth thee."*

Jacob's father at once demands whom he has blessed and confirms his blessing once the two brothers reveal it to him.

> *"Who then," he says, "hath hunted me venison, and brought it me, and I have eaten of all before thou camest, and have blessed him, and he shall be blessed."*

Thus, a divine blessing was given to the son who was favored and did the will of his father. Jacob's father sent him out into the land to find a wife so God may bless him, increase him, and multiply him, and become an assembly of the people where he dwells and inherits the land. On his journey, he received in a dream an oracle:

> *"And he came to a place and slept there, for the sun was set; and he took of the stones of the place, and put them at his head, and slept in that place, and dreamed. And behold a ladder set up on the earth, and the top of it reached to heaven; and the angels of God ascended and descended by it. And the Lord stood above it, and said, I am the God of Abraham the father, and the God of Isaac; fear not: the land whereon thou sleepest, to thee will I give it, and to thy seed; and thy seed shall be as the dust of the earth; and it shall be spread abroad to the sea, and to Africa, and to the north, and to the east: and all the tribes of the earth shall be blessed in thee and in they seed. And, behold, I am with thee, to keep thee in all thy way wherever thou goest, and I will bring thee back into this land; for I will not leave thee, until I have done all which I have spoken thee of. And Jacob awoke out of his sleep, and said, surely the Lord is in this place, and I knew it not. And he was afraid, and said, How dreadful is this place! This is none other but the house of God, and this is the gate of heaven. And Jacob arose, and took the stone that he had put under his head there, and set it up*

for a memorial, and poured oil upon the top of it. And Jacob called the name of that place the house of God."

This is the oracle sign given from the Spiritual World of the Divine to the Temporal World of mortal men. It was a significant moment indeed for Jacob, also called Israel (meaning seeing God). In Jacob's biblical story a spiraling ladder comes down from heaven and at the foot of this divine ladder lay a foundation witness stone which he laid his head upon. This is Jacob's pillar stone found in the desert which would witness all the Judah crowned kings in the future including Edward I Plantagenet. The regal chair holding the pillar stone was offered to St. Edward the Confessor in 1297. The British throne called Jacob's Pillar Stone, "the Coronation Stone," the Scottish throne called it the "Stone of Scone", and their cousins in North Ireland having once the same stone under their thrones called it the "Lia Fail – Bethel Stone." Jacob placed the original pillar stone in Bethel, the land of Canaan, and the modern state of Israel. It is said to be oblong of about twenty-two inches in length, thirteen inches broad, and eleven inches deep and of steel color mixed with some veins of red. Traditionally it is said to have been Jacob's pillow when he saw the angels of Bethel.

The oracle to Jacob is significant in how it parallels two events of the period. His travel to Egypt with Judah to be with his son Joseph bringing the pillar stone to Egypt at the same time as the acceptance of the oracle (priests) in Egypt and their rise to becoming Pharaoh. Jacob's journey to Egypt was during the reign of Thutmose III between 1700-1650 BC (Eighteenth Dynasty). This was a period of famine in regions outside of Egypt, battles in the Phoenician region by the Pharaoh, and great honors achieved by Joseph. The Pharaoh received Jacob with favor in Egypt, and he lived in Goshen until his death there. He was given an Egyptian style embalming and brought back to his former land by Joseph to be buried. The name of Jacob can be found by inscriptions in both the Palestinian region captured by Thutmose III and at Karnak in Egypt in the form of *Ya'kobh-el* (Jacob-el) *and Yoseph-el.* The favor given to Jacob could be in regards to his son Joseph and his significant encounter with an oracle from God. The latter was also of significant importance to Thutmose III, who was a priest in the temple of Amun at Karnak and rose to become Pharaoh. This was due to the oracle priests who lifted him there during the reign of Pharaoh Thutmose II and his wife Hatshepsut. The Pharaoh created a large empire through campaigns reaching as far as Syria while building fifty temples in Egypt. Both the annals at Karnak and the entries in the Pharaoh "day-book" from the kings' house show the holy war that raged during this period. Thutmose III believed his father Amun granted him the rights to foreign lands due to attacks upon Egypt. He made his tallies of victories in both the "day-book" and Karnak. The Pharaoh declared Amun gave him the justification and victory in extending the frontiers. Confiscating cities were not the only property he sought as he brought into his possession noble families creating a control mechanism throughout the frontier. This was in the time of Jacob and his son Judah. The oracle in Egypt was now formally represented and also rewarded by the new Pharaoh in Egypt. The two oracles with two different origins, one in Bethel and one in Amun in Karnak, had now met. They would both bring the oracle to the people and become powerful forces within Egypt and Greece for centuries to come. Jacob would pass the great honor of the origin of the oracle and his royal bloodline to his son Judah and grandson Zarah, who would both become known by many ancient traditions as Zeus.

Jacob had 12 sons and each of these sons formed a tribe in Israel. These were Reuben, Shimon, Levi, Judah, Issachar, Zebulun, Dan, Naphtali, Gad, Asher, Joseph, and Benjamin. These tribes settled on both sides of the Jordan

River and were known to history as the 12 Tribes of Israel. During this time as Jacob was dying in Egypt he blessed his son Judah.

> *"Judah, thy brethren thy praise thee: thy hands shall be on the back of thine enemy; thy father's children shall adore thee. Judah is a lion's whelp: from the sprouting, my son, thou art gone up: lying down, thou hast slept as a lion, and as a lion's whelp; who shall awake him? A prince shall not be lacking out of Judah, and a leader from his thighs, until the things come that are laid up for him; and He shall be the expectation of the nations. Binding his foal unto the vine, and his ass's foal to the choice vine; he shall wash red with wine, and his teeth are whiter than milk."*

Thus, the lion roared saying Judah alone has the power of laying down his life and the power of taking it again. He alone has the power of raising the temple once it has been destroyed. Moreover, it is Jacob who gave the promises to Judah that he is the expectation of the nations, and princes shall never be lacking of him. This is the sign that Jacob gave Judah the scepter and lawmaking as inheritance. There are biblical passages that declare Judah to be the lion's whelp and is likened to three lions, a grapevine, and possession of the scepter. Thus, the scepter is styled in biblical history in which Judah and all his descendants shall prevail, by which the chief ruler (prince) shall come.

The will of God is done through his children on earth as Noah and Abraham did the will of God. The scepter lineage began when Jacob accepted his father's decision to journey outward and finds God in the form of a dream and then passes it on to his son Judah who does his father's will. Both Jacob and Judah made God's will through their father's their own will by which they were greatly rewarded, prospered and multiplied. The heritage given down is both human and divine in that the son may succeed his father and become lawful possessor of inheritance and that of choice of divine right among the legal posterity of the heritage holder. The promise given would spread abroad from North, South, East, and West not only by race creating many nations but also a royal family that holds the scepter the emblem and sign of royalty.

The journey of Zarah is also part of the biblical story of Jacob of Israel and his connection with a Pillar Stone in the desert. This is the stone that would become the witness to all future king thrones of Judah and Israel. The sons of Judah are Er, Onan, Shelah, Pharah, and Zarah. Er and Onan died in the land of Canaan. The story of Zarah is about the Zarah Hebrew tribes of Judah whose wife Tamar bore twins. Zarah revealed his right hand, of which a scarlet thread or cord was tied around the wrist. His twin brother Pharah, however, would be born first. Thus, his brother Pharah would steal his brother's birthright by coming out of the womb first. Pharah becomes the messianic bloodline, the golden lion nation of Judah, and Zarah becomes the Gaelic Christian bloodline or scarlet lion nations of Judah. The descendants of Zarah are the Trojan, Spartan, Gaelic tribes that go back over 1,400 years before Christ.

The tribe of Zarah fled out of Egypt before the great exodus by Moses' Hebrew tribe under the Pharaoh Ramses. Zarah's journey started when he and his tribe moved out of the land of Egypt and across the coast of the Mediterranean to the Aegean Sea and up into the Black Sea. The Zarah tribes transformed themselves over 2,000 years from the ancient tribes of the Mediterranean to the pre-Catholic kings of Western Europe. The biblical sons of Zarah were Zimri, Ethan, Heman, Calcol, and Darda (Dardanus) five of them in all. Chalcol established the great city of Athens, Dardanus established Troy, and a Zimri established the eastern Black Sea. Through these three sons nurtured and fathered the nations of ancient Mediterranean area and Europe. The other tribes and factions of Zarah moved from the Greek isles and the Black Sea by land north or up the Danube River. These three sons of Zarah, however, are the most notable in history who carried on to do great things for the populace and journey abroad consolidating their culture, religion, and royal administration.

The migration of the Zarah tribes are put into three groups and two main migration routes. The first group is Chalcol sons who become the Milesians, Hyksos (Egyptian), Iberian (Spain), Irish and Scots tribes who made their migrations by ocean. The second group comes out of Dardanus' sons that become the Trojans, Celts, Franks, Scandinavia, and part of the British Isles. The third group came out of Zimri and Colchis' sons who become the Scythian/Scots, Saxon, and Suebians of Scandinavia that migrated by land north and west into Europe. They all could speak and understand different variations of the Gaelic language with its roots being Hebrew. Therefore from Zarah, God multiplied and spread across the lands of the Mediterranean and Europe and in each a royal prince made of his descendants.

The question that needs to be revealed is who were Judah and Zarah. Biblically they are the descendants of Jacob out of Israel, but to the ancient world before Christ they were much more. The discovery by the ancient Phoenician historian Sanchuniathon, who lived around the 1200 B.C, tried to make sense of this issue. It must be recognized that all material from Sanchuniathon is derived from the works of Philo of Byblos (flourished 100 AD) who claimed to have translated his Phoenicia from the original text. Some have questioned the authenticity of that claim, but excavations at Ras Shamra (ancient Ugarit) in Syria in 1929 revealed Phoenician documents supporting much of Sanchuniathon information on Phoenician mythology and religious beliefs. The writings of Sanchuniathon mention the Greek

Kronos, whom the Phoenicians call "Israel". Israel was the new name given to the biblical patriarch Jacob. The Phoenician historian further explained that this Kronos or Israel had a special son named Jehud or Yehud. This is simply a shortened form of the Hebrew Yehudah or Judah. The primary son of the Greek Kronos (Roman Saturn) was Zeus (Roman Jupiter), therefore, Jehud would be the same as Zeus. The word Zeus may actually derive from Yehud as the Roman Jupiter, as it appears to derive from the Greek Zeus-pater or Zheut-pater. Zheut meaning "akin" to a common bloodline (Hebrew) and "pater" meaning father. In the Aeneid by Virgil the word Jupiter is synonymous with Zeus. Therefore one can surmise that the following names are synonymous with both Hebrew and Phoenician names as Isaac (Uranus), Jacob (Kronos, Saturn), Judah (Jupiter, Zeus), and Zarah (Zeus). This is the Phoenician explanation of name terminology but it is muddled in ancient beliefs and pagan ideas. Thus, it must be looked at from another standpoint that merits logical terminology of the period.

The period in which Judah lived was a time of famine and attacks by the Egyptian Pharaoh, who in victories recorded on the wall at Karnak expected tribute and sons of leaders given as hostages for his rewards. Judah, known to the Phoenicians as Jupiter and also known as Zeus the Olympian in Greece, left for the Mediterranean region. Judah is given the name of Zeus the Olympian probably due to his great feats there as well as being the father of the Hebrew royal bloodline after Jacob. He is portrayed by the Titans (Teitan) in the same manner as others he is descended from. Isaac (Uranus) married Gaea (Ge, "earth goddess"), son Jacob (Kronos "god of heavens") married Rhea ("the gazer"). These names given to the biblical ones were used to signify a priest of the sun "heavens" or the traits one portrayed used over time since Adam and Eve. The Titans were considered adversaries to the Egyptians. Judah (Jupiter, Zeus) married two Pleiades, Maia (eldest) and Taygete, who were the daughters of Atlas (Epher) Kittim (Teitan), grandson of Abraham told by Josephus, and Pleione (Amazon). His son Zarah (Zeus) married Electra Roma a Pleiade and also a daughter of Atlas. Judah the lion and the builder of nations could for this reason surmised as also being Zeus the Olympian and father of many as Jacob foretold in his blessing.

The reasoning for Zarah as being Zeus is in the understanding that Zarah is the father of Dardanus as well as many others that inhabited the Mediterranean region of ancient times. Zeus in the "Iliad" by Homer is said to be by lineage the father of Dardanus. This would make the Phoenician name of Zeus synonymous with the biblical name of Zarah. Both Judah and Zarah would be well known in the ancient region of Greece and Egypt since they lived there under the Pharaoh's and were the fathers of many children as tabulated (see Zeus: Wives, Consorts, and Children). The name Zeus or

Zheut-pater (pater meaning "father") would be synonymous with a high ranking, almost worshipped type man. He was looked upon for guidance and security over all the mortal and in some beliefs immortal offspring. A final important point is that if one explores the language the word Zheut means akin or bloodline to a common peoples, in this case the Israelites and pater meaning "highest order" or "father". Therefore, Zeus is the father of the bloodline as witnessed in ancient times by the Egyptians and the tribes that made up the Mediterranean area. One can explore these facts or pagan beliefs to many depths, but the main reality is the genealogical bloodline has been recorded over time asserting to the migration of the tribes from Jacob to the Mediterranean area during this time period.

Zarah marrying Electra Roma, who is a daughter of a Titan Atlas (Epher) Kittim, finds the final point in this resolution. Zarah being the father of many and kin to Titans would make him the most likely person to be Zeus. A great deal of Babylonian paganism was overlaid onto these historical characters, creating the false gods of Greek and Roman mythology. A number of royal genealogies based on Homer describe the descent of Trojan royalty as follows: Zeus – Dardanus – Erichthonius – Tros – Ilus – Laomedon – Priam. While this lineage might appear mythical, we should note that some ancient myths about the "gods" were actually rooted in stories about real people. In fact, many pagan religions began, in part, as ancestral hero worship. Thus from the line of Pharah came the royal house of David, while from the Zarah line came the royal house of Troy.

Zeus had many marriages and consorts. A list of some of them and the children of each are as follows: Dione (Aphrodite), Hera (Ares), Leto (Apollo, Artemis), Metis (Athena), Mnemoysne (Muses), Alcmene (Heracles), Electra Roma (Dardanus), Europa (Sarpedon), Pyrrha (Hellen). Electra Roma was the Pleiade Star or Mountain Nymph of Mount Saon on the island of Samothrake in the Greek Aegean off the coast where Troy would later be built. Electra Roma was the daughter of Pleione, Queen of the Amazons, who had six other daughters by Atlas (Epher) Kittim in Maia, Taygete, Alcyone, Celaeno, Sterope, and Merope. She fell in love with Zarah (Zeus) and bore him two sons, Dardanus, ancestor of the Trojan royal family and Iasion, founder of the Samothrakian Mysteries. Electra Roma was known as the bright or brilliant one, a daughter of Atlas (Epher) Kittim and Pleione as she was one of the seven Pleiades. She is connected also with the legend about the Palladium. Electra Roma had come as a supplicant to the Palladium, which Athena had established. Zeus or Athena herself had thrown it into the territory of Ilium because it had been sullied by the hands of a woman who was no longer a pure maiden and there King Ilus built a temple to Zeus. According to others, it was Electra Roma herself that brought the Palladium to Ilium and gave it to her son Dardanus. When she saw the city of her son perishing in flames she tore out her hair in grief and was thus placed among the stars as a comet. Other stories told how Electra Roma and her six sisters were placed among the stars as the seven Pleiades and lost their brilliancy on seeing the destruction of Ilium. This would not, however, be the end of Ilium or what would later become the great city of Troy. It was rebuilt many times over and the fate of it would be of the will of Zeus.

Zarah (Zeus), son Dardanus would be the ancestor of the Trojan royal family but he would not be alone in the impact made upon the ancient Troy, the Greeks, and the Mediterranean region. Hercules, blessed with great strength, was a favorite son of Zeus. His strength was necessary in his travels to the Far East, the same taken up by Jason and then Alexander the Great. Apollo was blessed with divine wisdom in both virtuous and pious living. He is known for slaying the evil python that dwelt amongst the Greek lands. The very place where he slew the python would be built the oracle of Delphi in his name. The Trojans would build their own temple to him hoping he would protect and give them wisdom that would make for a prosperous lifestyle. Aphrodite was blessed with beauty and a son named Aeneas who would become a great captain of the Trojans and the founder of the Romans. Athena was blessed with warrior abilities, which she would used to aid in turning the fortunes of battle in favor of those she cherished the most. Hellen was also blessed with beauty for which many men sought to win her hand in marriage. She would both marry and turn away many men and for this became the center of an epic war between the ancestors and children of Zeus. The blessing onto Judah from his father Jacob came to pass as shown by these children of Zeus, and the son has done his father's will and the will of God.

The scepter of Judah (Zeus) was used to transform his will and the will of God to mortal men. Insight from ancient texts and people who lived during these ancient times support this idea. The following insights by others of the time may give the needed understanding of the divine workings of Zeus. The poems of Homer in the "Iliad" are the first and most detailed accounts of the will of Zeus throughout the Trojan and Greek regions during the Trojan War. Homer describes in his poems about the Trojan War how the gods and Zeus are in a bitter struggle for the cause and prosperity of the mortals they cherish the most and the outcome the gods prefer. Zeus is the supreme and highest ranking god amongst the gods (Titans) and is in constant turmoil in appeasing the other gods while keeping to his design plan. Zeus is the father to many in both Troy and in Greece and some of the gods (Teitan) produced the offspring of these two great regions. Zeus cherishes his children as does Apollo, the protectorate of the Trojans, his son from Leo and both are joined in aiding the city of Troy and the Trojan people. The lines are drawn between the gods (Teitan) in this great story and only Zeus can transform what is wrong to right and what is not just to just as he will for centuries to come.

In the most crucial part of the battle in Homer's "Iliad" Zeus calls upon all the gods to assemble on top of Mount Olympus to lay down before them his final decision on the matter of intervention upon the mortals thrown into battle. Zeus lets the gods know who is the supreme god by first saying:

> *"Hear me," said he, "gods and goddesses,that I may speak even as I am minded. Let none of you neithergoddess nor god try to cross me, but obey me every one of youthat I may bring this matter to an end. If I see anyone actingapart and helping either Trojans or Danaans, he shall be beateninordinately ere he come back again to Olympus; or I will hurlhim down into dark Tartarus far into the deepest pit under theearth, where the gates are iron and the floor bronze, as farbeneath Hades as heaven is high above the earth, that you maylearn how much the mightiest I am among you. Try me and find outfor yourselves. Hangs me a golden chain from heaven, and lay holdof it all of you, gods and goddesses together--tug as you will,you will not drag Jove the supreme counselor from heaven toearth; but were I to pull at it myself I should draw you up withearth and sea into the bargain, then would I bind the chain aboutsome pinnacle of Olympus and leave you all dangling in the midfirmament. So far am I above all others either of gods or men."*

Zeus decreed his will upon the gods and to the mortals drawn to battle. The gods are obedient to the will of Zeus but also seek to alter his decisions by appeals, bringing up past faithfulness, and adoration. Hera appeals to him to be lenient upon the Achaean's while Athena, Ares, and Poseidon plot their next step in the aftermath of these orders of Zeus. Zeus then harnessed up his most illustrious battle-car and armor and went his way to his altar upon the slopes of Mount Ida. There he assumed his throne in all its glory and looked out upon the walls of Troy and the armies of Achaea. There he put forth the fates of the Trojans and the Achaeans, all armed in bronze, by sending down a crash of thunder and bolts of lightning unto the Achaeans. This took them all back into a horrific state while lifting the spirits of Troy. After some time of battle the Trojans were pinned against the walls of Troy. It was then that Zeus sent down another example of his power by a crash of thunder and a bolt of lightning unto the battle cars and feet of the Achaeans, splitting the earth in front of them. Nestor cries to Diomedes:

> *"All had then been lost and no help for it, for they would havebeen penned up in Ilius like sheep, had not the sire of gods andmen been quick to mark, and hurled a fiery flaming thunderboltwhich fell just*

*in front of Diomed's horses with a flare ofburning brimstone. The
horses were frightened and tried to backbeneath the car, while the
reins dropped from Nestor's hands.Then he was afraid and said to
Diomed, "Son of Tydeus, turn yourhorses in flight; see you not that
the hand of Jove is againstyou? To-day he vouchsafes victory to Hector;
to-morrow, if it soplease him, he will again grant it to ourselves; no
man, howeverbrave, may thwart the purpose of Jove, for he is far
strongerthan any."*

The tide would turn throughout the battle from one great foe to the next
only by the intervening of the other gods not in favor of Zeus great plan. The
gods in favor of the Trojans and the city of Troy do what they can to protect
it from destruction and afterward lay the groundwork for its restoration.
Aphrodite aids in the protection of her son in the "Iliad" allowing Aeneas to
survive a battle with Achilles and soon after he follows the will of Zeus in his
journey to Italy. Apollo, builder of the city of Troy, aids the Trojans with his
bow and arrow and with Poseidon after its fall help to clear the destruction
for rebuilding. The Trojans, who would be led by Helenus, in this rebuilding
did the will of Zeus and brought it to all followers by the oracle of Dodona.

The final turning point came when Zeus made a decision that would
effect not only the great figures of this story but later ones as well. The fate
of the Trojans will come by the will of Achilles and his fate by the will of
Zeus, thus justice to both will be done by Zeus who inherited the scepter
and lawmaking from Judah the lion. This is the arrangement in the "Iliad"
when Achilles is sparring off with Argememnon, who is really in charge of the
troops fighting against the Trojan's. Achilles attacks his authority by saying
Argememnon does not put on his armor or fight with his army while at the
same time destroying it, which disgraces him. He makes an oath by Zeus'
scepter that the Achaea army will be crying for his aid once the man killing
Hector has cut down his share of Achaean's.

*"But the son of Peleus again began railing at the son of Atreus,for he
was still in a rage. "Wine-bibber," he cried, "with theface of a dog and
the heart of a hind, you never dare to go outwith the host in fight, nor
yet with our chosen men in ambuscade.You shun this as you do death
itself. You had rather go round androb his prizes from any man who
contradicts you. You devour yourpeople, for you are king over a feeble
folk; otherwise, son ofAtreus, henceforward you would insult no man.
Therefore I say,and swear it with a great oath--nay, by this my scepter
whichshalt sprout neither leaf nor shoot, nor bud anew from the day
onwhich it left its parent stem upon the mountains--for the axestripped
it of leaf and bark, and now the sons of the Achaeansbear it as judges*

and guardians of the decrees of heaven--sosurely and solemnly do I swear that hereafter they shall lookfondly for Achilles and shall not find him. In the day of yourdistress, when your men fall dying by the murderous hand ofHector, you shall not know how to help them, and shall rend yourheart with rage for the hour when you offered insult to thebravest of the Achaeans."

This is the will of Achilles to win him honor and glory for the ages in contempt of his king. The great warrior has now set the stage for glory but there would be a price to pay, which would be the will of Zeus, who would uphold justice over one's glory. Achilles sends his mother, the goddess Thetis, to go talk this over with Zeus to gain his favor and then Zeus hands down his will to Achilles the price to pay for his grand plan and eternal glory. Thus Thetis goes to Mount Olympus and begs Zeus for Achilles' plan to happen. Then with a bit of outrage of taking sides with the Trojans against the other gods he bows his head in agreement that it shall happen.

"I shall have trouble if you set me quarreling with Juno, for she will provoke me with her taunting speeches; even now she is always railing atme before the other gods and accusing me of giving aid to theTrojans. Go back now, lest she should find out. I will considerthe matter, and will bring it about as you wish. See, I inclinemy head that you may believe me. This is the most solemn promisethat I can give to any god. I never recall my word, or deceive,or fail to do what I say, when I have nodded my head."

The price set for this great victory over the Trojans and the bringing down of Hector, prince of Troy, would be great for Achilles. Soon after this, he would be brought down in battle and never see his fellow Achaeans sail back to Greece.

The reasoning behind the fall of Troy as the will of Zeus can only be found in the divine will of God. If one looks backward and forward in time on the city of Troy from the time this epic story took place, it will be found that the citadel of Troy was built and destroyed many times. The blessing from Jacob to Judah thus is brought to pass through Zarah. The lion roared, saying he alone has the power of laying down his life and the power of taking it again. He alone has the power of raising the temple once it has been destroyed. The glory of one over the other is not outweighed by the justice of the other and continuation of the divine journey and will of God. Hector the prince of Troy and the main hope to save the city fights a courageous battle whose tides turn several times. He attempts to subdue the friend of Achilles before reaching the walls of Troy and finally brings down Patroclus. This in turn brings Achilles out of his camp to meet Hector man to man in the final duel before the destruction of Troy. Hector the prince only seeks to bring his people home, be with his family, and prosper. Achilles seeks glory and fame at the price of certain death. The warrior, with his armor crafted by the gods, could not be subdued by the fighting spirit and strength of Hector but this would not be the last time these two great adversaries in would meet on this very ground.

The wall and trench that was built by the Achaeans to defend their ships was built against the will of Zeus, Poseidon, and Apollo. When the battle was over and the Achaeans left with their ships the gods joined together by Zeus ordered to cause the rivers from Mount Ida to crash upon the gates while rain poured for nine days. The battle armor, foundations and beams that littered the land were washed away leaving a smooth plain, which vanished all remnants of the war. This was the will of Zeus.

The origins of the oracle temples in Greece are said to have come by way of Egypt upon the contention of Herodotus. He states that the Phoenicians carried off two oracle priestesses from Thebes as slaves and brought them to Lybia (Amun) and Greece (Zeus). They drew the attention of their owners to their abilities and founded shrines in both locations. The location of the oracle in Greece was Dodona, the oldest known oracle in the Mediterranean. The priestess there built a shrine to Zeus under an oak tree. There the priestess gave her oracles by the wind that blew through the mountain valley and rustled the oak leaves. The establishment of the oracle of Zeus was sometime around the thirteenth century BC and evolved over time.

The oracle of Dodona lies in the region known as Epirus on the west of the Greek mainland. It is from here that the origin of the Zeus oracle begins with the worship of the sacred oak. This oracle or sacred oak worship was taken up by the earth goddess Ge (Gaea) and then the cult of Zeus in the thirteenth century. In Delphi, an oracle established there had a similar history. The goddess Ge was the first to begin the oracle and pass it on to her daughter Themis, then to Phoebe the daughter of Uranus and Ge. Finally, Apollo took possession of it from his mother, Leto, daughter of Phoebe. Another story states that Apollo killed the Python who guarded the oracle for Ge with a bow and arrow and won possession of it. The interesting point here is the Phoenician names again. Uranus (Isaac) and Ge had by marriage Kronos (Jacob) and Phoebe, then they have respected children of Zeus (Judah) and Leto, who are the parents of Apollo. The names for the gods at the oracle are said to have come from Homer and Hesiod, which was learned by Herodotus from and oracle priestesses at Dodona.

The Trojans and ancient Greeks looked to Zeus and Apollo for guidance in all areas of life. The Trojans built a temple to Apollo and had priests, priestess and seers translate the signs. Apollo the protector of Troy was the main counsel to Zeus in the campaign to save Troy from destruction. He intervened in the mortal battle many times with his bow and shield. Apollo was the divine messenger for the Trojans to Zeus. It was thought that if one did the will of Zeus one would prosper as did the Trojans. The Greeks soon came to adopt this idea in the form of oracles in Dodona and Delphi. Dodona was an oracle for Zeus while Delphi was and oracle to Apollo. Each in its own way was highly respected and prosperous among the people of the time. The oracles were built as temples with priests and priestess selected to perform and deliver divine messages. One could travel to the temples to get guidance on many topics that were of importance to them. The areas sought out by individuals for guidance ranged from, marriages, farming, military, government, and legal matters (justice). The oracle was relied upon to give accurate messages and in doing so became a popular tool for those who wished to draw upon its wisdom. These oracles were so valued for their position as a messenger for Zeus and Apollo that they existed up to 300 AD. Zeus was relied upon for many generations and followed throughout the Mediterranean region.

There were seven predominant oracles within the Greek region, which brought the messages of Apollo and Zeus to the people. The oracles at Delphi, Abae, and Didyma were built in honor of Apollo and shared his divine messages and his divine way of living through both priest and priestess. The oracles at Dodona and Siwa (Libyan Desert) were built in honor of Zeus. The former is the one Helenus of Troy was known to have been a priest at after the fall of the city of Troy and the latter is where the priestess of Amun foretold the future. Two other oracles were at Oropus held by a priest named Amphiaraus, supposedly a son of Apollo, and Lebadea, chosen also for the son of Apollo, Trophonius. There were many other oracles within the Mediterranean region, each with its vast visitors and wealth, showing the divine will of Apollo and Zeus was greatly accepted and followed. The existence of this following is shown by the fact that not only did the common people seek these messages but also kings of regions and Empires like Croesus of Lydia in 560 BC and Xerxes of Persia in 480 BC. The oracles allowed the people to stay connected with what they valued most, which was their ancestors (bloodline to the "father" Zeus) and justice handed down by the divine.

The system for giving the divine messages was similar for all the oracles. There was a high priest or priestess that was selected for a one year period of time to take written messages from the day prior to the oracle to be answered in their own divine way. A fee was usually presented at the time of submitting written messages, which were put in a jar and given to the high priest or priestess. Before the time of divine messages to be given out, the oracles in some cases would participate in rituals including fasts, baths, and lengthy meditation. The treasury, stadium, and adytum were the main building within the oracle site.

There was a consensus among the people of the time that if one prayed to Zeus and followed the will of Zeus justice would always follow. Hesiod, a farmer and poet in Greece about 700 BC, would become the Greeks' great authority on the immortal gods due to his divine vision with the gods. One day while shepherding his lambs under Mount Helicion the Muses of Olympus and daughters of Zeus came upon him in a thick mist to give him a message from the gods and Zeus.

> *"Muses of Pieria who give glory through song, come hither,tell of Zeus your father and chant his praise. Through him mortal menare famed or un-famed, sung or unsung alike, as great Zeus wills. Foreasily he makes strong, and easily he brings the strong man low; easilyhe humbles the proud and raises the obscure, and easily he straightensthe crooked and blasts the proud,--Zeus who thunders aloft and has hisdwelling most high.Attend thou with eye and ear, and make judgments straight with righteousness. And I, Perses, would tell of true things."*

In addition, the daughters of Zeus plucked and gave him a rod wrapped with laurel and then breathed into him the voice to celebrate things that shall be and things that were to be afterwards. Then they had him sing the race of the blessed gods that are eternal. The ability to see through the mist and take the rod allowed Hesiod the right to speak with a divine voice, which was the will of the gods yet to be. His poems describe the origins of the world, the gods, and rural life

The two things Hesiod taught his fellow Greeks were to work upon work that is ordained to men and to abstain from what is given to the fishes and beasts, which is to devour one another, but instead what was given to mankind which proves to be right. The gods have given goodness to man by the sweat of his brows and thus man needs to work the work ordained them. This manner of life spread from city to city in the Mediterranean area led the Greeks to an inspired life instead of being wretched creatures. They would learn to die gloriously and live righteously. The law of Zeus even in the midst of war, oppression, and slavery would fill the hearts of man.

Greece found itself against a great adversary in the Persian Empire and found a leader inspired by the divine the will of Zeus to become victorious. Alexander the Great of Macedonia would seek out justice, live a divine life, create unity among many, be merciful to his enemies, build a great empire, and decline worship. He would become the symbol of Zeus' will in ancient times. He believed himself to be the son of Zeus as did many others of his time. The characteristics he possessed where cunning, political shrewdness, morality, spirit, grace. All these traits would allow him to unite the people and employ wisdom and force to spread his ideas and conquer the longtime enemies who brought war upon them. Alexander the Great used dreams, words, and prayers to Zeus to guide in this task that not even Philip his father had taken upon himself. Alexander created and empire and was Lord of Asia and justice had been done for his people that were in the past constantly under strife by the Persian Empire. The son of Zeus as he was thought to be had brought the will of Zeus to all men under the common law and dream he had set forth as a student of Aristotle in Macedonia.

Alexander founded the first of many cities to be named Alexandria during a campaign that led from Gaza to Egypt. A respectful gesture was given during these travels to the divine in front of the people at the Oasis of Amun, an oracle similar to the ones in Dodona and Delphi. Amun is the Egyptian name for Zeus and the Greeks identified Amun with Zeus. This visit signified Alexander to be the will of the people bestowed upon him by the will of Zeus.

The Great Macedonian King would also cross the plain of Troy to visit Ilium (Troy) and give sacrifices and libations to the Temple of Athene, Temple of Zeus, and Priam. He set his armor in the temple and gave honor to all the ancient heroes while exchanging arms that had been kept from the Trojan War to help lead his men in battle.

The will of Zeus echoed through the ages and to show their honor for him a temple was built at Olympia and was finished in 457 BC. The temple was known for the thirty-eight doric columns that enclosed the statue of Zeus with a scepter in one hand and Victory in the other made of wooden core overlaid with gold, silver and ivory. The statue was known as one of the Seven Wonders of the World and was taken to Constantinople in 393 AD where it was destroyed in a fire.

The will of God descended upon Jacob in the form of a ladder of angels, then to Judah (Zeus) in the form of a blessing, and then upon Zarah (Zeus) through birthright of the scarlet thread. Each did the will of God thus creating the beginning of the royal lineage of Judah Scepter. The descendants of Zarah (Zeus) would follow the will of their father by a race of people called the Trojans who came from the ancient city of Troy. This race of people would be resilient, religious, and prosperous despite the confrontations imposed upon them and their city over the centuries. The justice handed down by Zeus would enable them to overcome the destruction caused by wars and rebuild their city in more grandeur than the previous. After the fall of Troy the connection to the will of Zeus would continue by oracles, texts (poems), kings, and the descendants of Troy who migrated to Europe and settled in the upper Rhine area. A new temple established there in honor of Zeus and a new race of people would begin. Justice had been done as the royal lineage found a new homeland to prosper, multiply, and grow as children of Zeus and God. The blessing of the words unto Judah would bring forth the building of many nations and the laws to govern them.

II

TROJAN

Draw nigh the seer, and strive with prayers to have her holy tale;
Beseech her sing, and that her words from willing tongue go free:
So reverenced shall she tell thee tale of folk of Italy and wars to
come; and how to escape, and how to bear each ill, and with a
happy end at last thy wandering shall fulfill. Go, let thy deeds
Troy's mightiness exalt above the sky

Helenus, "The Aeneids of Virgil" by Virgil Book III

THE TROJANS WERE A great alliance of people whose kings descended by
birthright of the scarlet thread from Zarah (Zeus), holder of the royal scepter.
The foundation that the Trojan people are known for is the great citadel they
built in the same place over centuries time named Troy (Ilium). This city
prospered and had a great marketplace, royal living quarters, battle quarters,
and temples. It was heavily fortified due to its great wealth and prosperity and
had a great wall no enemy could overcome. The Trojans were also known for
their great battle strength, horse breeding and chariot (car) expertise. All these
areas would be found necessary in the wars they fought and to bring allies
together for fighting against masses of armies sent to destroy the city for its
riches. The Trojans would also rely upon the protector of the city, Apollo, and
his bow and arrows. The Trojans built a temple to Apollo and believed that
the way he lived should be the proper way to live in harmony with oneself and
nature. The Trojans were a grand alliance of people who shared in the wealth
throughout the region and sought to live by faith in God through those they
knew and loved as they built their temples to Zeus, Hera, and Apollo with
priests and seers to guide them to prosperity.

The founding of the city, known as Troy (Ilium), started with Dardanus
the son of Zarah according to the ancient Greek story the "Iliad" by Homer.
Dardanus' grandson, Tros, was the namesake of the ancient Trojans and of

their capital city of Troy. Tros had three sons, Ilus, Ganymede, and Assaracus. The reigning kings of the Trojans were of the line of Ilus. Aeneas, founder of the Roman Empire, was a prince of the royal house of Assaracus.

Dardanus was a son of Zarah (Zeus) and Electra Roma, daughter of Atlas (Epher) Kittim. He was the founder of Dardania, a city on Mount Ida in the Troad. Iasius and Dardanus were the two brothers who lived in Samothrake an island off Greece in the northern Aegean Sea. The name of the island means Thracian Samos and it is only a few kilometres west of Turkey in the maritime boundary between Greece. Dardanus was from Arcadia, where he and his elder brother Iasius reigned as kings following Atlas (Epher) Kittim. Dardanus married Chryse daughter of Pallas by whom he fathered two sons Idaeus and Dymas. A great flood occurred causing the survivors, who were living on mountains that had now become islands, to split into two groups. One group remained and took Dymas as king while the other sailed away eventually settling on the island of Samothrace. Iasius was slain by Zeus for lying with Demeter while Dardanus and his people found the land poor and so most of them set sail for Asia. They took up their abode at the foot of Mount Ida, calling the city Dardania, which at the time was ruled by Teucer. However, there was a story that Dardanus and Iasius originally came from Hesperia, ("evening land", or "western land"), which was afterward renamed as Italy. In the Aeneid by Virgil it is foretold by Helenus to Aeneas, who at the time was seeking to travel to Italy after the Trojan war, that this was the true home of Dardanus and Isasius.

Dardanus came to the Troad from Samothrace and was there welcomed by King Teucer and married his daughter Batea, the daughter of Teucer. Dardanus first wife Chryse had died. Teucer, son of the river god Scamander and the nymph Idaea, was then king of that country and the people were called Teucrians after him. King Teucer welcomed the foreigner and gave him his daughter Batea as a wife, and also a share of his land. Dardanus thus received land on Mount Ida from his father-in-law and founded a city in the region that later was called the Troad. There he lived with his family until the death of his father-in-law, upon which he became king of the whole land and called it Dardania after himself. Dardanus' children by Batea were Ilus, Erichthonius, and Idaeus. Dardanus' son Idaeus gave his name to the Idaean mountains, that is Mount Ida, where Idaeus built a temple to the Mother of the Gods and instituted mysteries and ceremonies observed in Phrygia.

To completely understand the region during this time a view of serveral forces upon it must be looked at in a broader way. The Egyptians, Hittites, Amazons, Phoenicians, Teucerian (Tekkri), Javan, and all the dominions of the Troad were all expanding and contracting upon the region known as Asia Minor. The Egptians under the Pharaoh Ramses II (1333 BC) and Ramses

III were being invaded by the Teucerians and internally struggling with an uprising amongst the Hebrews under Moses. These uprisings against the Egptians would bring it into decline while Asia Minor would now begin to flourish after struggles with the Pharaoh Thutmose III. The Hittite Empire was at its height in the fourteenth century (BC) in the area of Anatolia, which emcompasses northwestern Syria and Turkey. They did battle with the Egyptians under Pharaoh Ramses II and aided the city of Troy by Memmon before their decline. The Amazons lived in the far eastern part of Phygia (Turkey) and tended to ally themselves only upon necessity. This can explain the consorts and marriages beteween Judah (Zeus) and Zarah (Zeus) with the Pleiones, who were Amazonian by Pleone. Finally, there is the Javan who were in general the Greek people in Asia Minor, also known as Ionians, who controlled the commerce in the East. These inhabitants made up the dominions of the Troad and interacted amongst each other and fought against the Egpytians.

The Dominions of the Troad are are made up of Trojans, which are divided into nine dominions Pandarus, the sons of Merops, Asius, Aeneas, Altes, Cilicians, Homeric Arimi, Pelasgians, and Priam (Ilium). The Pandarus Dominion were known to be very wealthy and were known as Lycians, named after his father Lycaon, an excellent archer. The sons of Merops' Dominion bordered the previous and were knonw as Milesians. The Asius Dominion was along the Troad coast of the Hellespont which included Thracian cities. The Aeneas Dominions included the Dardanians and was a narrow strip of plain on the side of Mount Ida. The Altes Dominion was father in law to Priam and the grandfather of Lycaon of the Pandarus Dominion. The Cicilian Dominions include the cities of Thebe and Chryse, which were destroyed in the Trojan War and more importantly where the Temple of Apollo had been built. The Homeric Arimi were a mythic people thought to be from the Lydia area. The Pelasgian Dominion occupied the area from the Aeolian coast to the Ionian frontier. Finally, the Priam (Ilium) Dominion encompassed the plain of Thymbra of which flowed the Scamander River and on this plain was the citadel of Illium. On the outlying areas are the Lycians, Mysians, and Phrygian who were breakers and breeders of horses. These are the Dominions of the Troad who were all considered Trojans being allied with each other throughout the ancient times from Thutmose III to the Trojan War against the armies of Agememnon. In this region were the beginnings of the royal bloodline from Zarah (Zeus) to Helenus and many centuries after the Trojan War as they built the great walls, palaces and temples to the gods in the citadel called Troy.

The Trojans and their names are associated with the Phrygians and Teucerians spoken of by both Herodotus and Homer. The Phrygians are associated with the Thracians, who were neighbors of the Macedonians who migrated to Asia Minor. The names of Hector, Hecuba, Alexander, Paris, and Scamadrios are considered to be Phrygian.

The royal bloodline continued when Dardanus died and his son Erichthonius inherited the royal scepter becoming the richest of men in both the kingdoms of his father and that of his maternal grandfather. Erichthonius married Astyoche, daughter of the river god Simois, a sister of Teucer. This marriage produced a son, Tros, who married Callirrhoe, and coming to the throne called the people Trojans, naming the land Troad. The founder of Troy was Ilus son of Tros who founded the city of Ilium (Troy) that he named after himself. Ilus went to Phrygia and took part in games that at the time were held by the king, winning a victory in wrestling. He received fifty youths and as many maidens as a prize. The king, obeying an oracle, gave him also a cow and asked him to found a city wherever the cow should lie down. The cow rested on the hill of Ate and in that spot Ilus built the city, which he called Ilium. Then he prayed to Zeus that a sign might be shown to him blessing this site. He saw the Palladium fallen from heaven and lying before his tent. Ilus was then blinded, for any man might not look upon the Palladium (Athene standing on a column). Later he made offerings to the goddess and recovered his sight. The kingdom of Dardanus and Erichthonius was divided when Ilus became king of Ilium (Troy) and his brother Assaracus continued to be king of the Dardanians. Ilus preferred his new city of Ilium to Dardania and on his father's death he remained there, bestowing the rule of Dardania on his brother Assaracus. Therefore, Tros had two sons, Ilus and Assaracus, which sprang two separate lines; Ilus, Laomedon, Priam, Helenus and Assaracus, Capys, Anchises, Aeneas. The Trojan War would unite these two royal lines and Helenus and Aeneas would fight alongside each other in battle and later would create the royal lines of two great empires.

Ilus had a son Laomedon who became king of Troy after him. When Laomedon was king of Troy, Apollo and Poseidon decided to put him to the test. Assuming the likeness of mortal men, the two gods undertook to fortify Troy by building the walls of Troy for wages. King Laomedon would not pay their wages when the work was done, so Apollo sent a pestilence, and Poseidon sent a sea-monster that snatched away the people of the plain. The oracles foretold deliverance from these calamities if Laomedon would expose his daughter Hesione to be devoured by the sea-monster. Obedient of this oracle he agreed with the gods and exposed Hesione to the monster by fastening her to the rocks near the sea. When Heracles saw her exposed he promised to save her on condition of receiving from Laomedon the mares which Zeus had given him. Again Laomedon promised to pay for the service and Heracles killed the monster and saved Hesione. When this was accomplished, however,

Laomedon would not give the agreed reward. Heracles besieged and took the city slaying Laomedon and his family. The life of Podarces, though, was spared at the request of Hesione on condition that Podarces first be a slave and then be redeemed by her. Hesione gave her veil for him and hence his name of Priam, Greek for "to buy". Priam after gaining his freedom first married Arisbe and then Hecuba, fathering fifty sons and twelve daughters. Among these sons were Hector, Paris, Helenus and among the daughters Polyxena and Cassandra. The inheritance of the royal scepter was given to the king of Troy as he multiplied by the blessing given unto Judah.

Troy was a well-fortified city with broad streets and beautiful palaces. Asian allies included the Ascanians, Amazons, Lycians, and the Eastern Ethiopians who came with their armies to help the besieged city when it became necessary. The city of Troy stood as a citadel overlooking the Hellespont for centuries. The memory of the correct location of Troy was lost to the ages by the first century AD. In the eighteenth century a French Antiquarian, Jean-Baptiste Lechevalierm went to Asia Minor and reported the site of Troy to be Bunarbashi due to observations of the two springs, one hot and one cold, that fed the Scammander river. This river was mentioned in Homer's "Iliad" during the Trojan War. Others came to the same conclusion due to the plains that existed in the area and the impregnable hill on which the fortress could be constructed. Then later the debate led to a new site, which was a few miles nearer to the coast and was called Hissarlik or Turkish for "fortress". A map of the area showed the rivers, marshes, brooks, and canals that made up the Troad. However, the only way to find the exact site of Troy was to excavate the area entirely. Was Homer a poet or a historian? It wasn't until 1870 that the legendary city of the Homeric poems was brought to light by a German archaeologist Heinrich Schliemann, who began excavations which uncovered the actual stone walls, battlements and treasures of the ancient city.

Schliemann's excavations at Hissarlik found many treasures and the actual foundations that made up the walls and rooms of Troy. The treasures found were supposedly collected by a family member or servant before the fateful period and then abandoned during departure of the burning city. The items included a statue of Apollo, large silver vases, gold earrings, bracelets, goblets, and thousands gold rings. The site brought forth the walls of Troy, which covered an oval space about two hundred yards from west to east and one hundred and seventy five yards from north to south. It comprised a citadel, not a city, protecting the house and homes of the nobility. Most people lived outside the walls near the eastern plateau. What Schliemann would find was five separate cities, and two more would follow one on top of the other to a depth of twenty yards. The palace of Priam had in its location terra-cotta vases filled with treasures of all kinds seemingly packed away and hidden during the fall of Troy.

Schliemann's assistant Wilhelm Dorpfeld continued work in this area after his death and then Blegen threw new and important light upon Schliemann's discoveries. The excavations at the mound of Hissarlik revealed successive settlements. TROY I is an early settlement with a wall built of small stones and clay dating back perhaps around 3000 BC destroyed by fire. TROY II is a prehistoric fortress with strong ramparts, a palace, and houses, dating from the third millennium BC whose inhabitants were craftsmen making goblets and jewelry. TROY III, IV, and V were prehistoric villages successively built on the debris of TROY II during the period from 2300 to 2000 BC which was the Bronze Age. TROY VI was a fortress including a larger area than any of the preceding settlements with huge walls, towers, gates, and houses dating from 1900 to 1300 BC whose inhabitants brought with them horses. TROY VIIA was a reconstruction of TROY VI built in the latter part of this period after an earthquake destroyed the city. TROY VIIB, VIII had Greek villages of simple stone houses dating from about 1100 BC to the first century BC. TROY IX was the acropolis of the Graeco-Roman city of Ilion or New Ilion with a temple of Athena, public buildings, and a large theater, which existed from the first century BC to about 500 AD. The various settlements noted above were located over a period of time by different parties of which Schliemann identified TROY II with the Homeric Troy discovered five. Dorpfeld's discoveries, however, seemed to indicate that the Homeric Troy must be identified with TROY VIIA, which was evidently destroyed by fire at the traditional date of the Trojan War. Some later authorities claim TROY VI with its massive battlements was the Troy of Homer, which carries some credence when all the facts are examined.

Over time, the walls of Troy rose higher and its surface area spread wider. The depths from the surface to the different settlements are six feet to Troy VII, six and half feet to Troy VI, thirteen feet to Troy V, twenty three feet to Troy IV, thirty three feet to Troy III, forty five feet to Troy II, and a final depth of fifty two and half feet to Troy I. The acropolis stood one hundred nine and a half feet above sea level and fifty-nine and half feet above the plain at the foot of the city. The city of Troy could thus be seen for many distances away in all directions within the plains of the Troad and was regarded as the capital city of The Trojan Dominions.

Troy was built of polished stone with fifty chambers for Priams' sons and daughters and twelve chambers for his sons and daughter in laws as well as separate dwellings for Hector and Paris with a great hall and court. The Temples of Athene, Apollo, and Zeus were within the city walls, which the Trojans considered a sacred place. A statue of Phoebus Apollo and doric columns were found along with the four horses of the Sun. A watchtower was also built within the city, which stood as an impenetrable place of Apollo, who shot his arrows on any armies who sought to besiege it. Another point of interest found by Schliemann is a small hill next to the acropolis which grew many fig trees as well as having several small mounds throughout the plain. These were considered to be burial sites with stone walls inside and the remains of what is considered to be that of Achilles, Patroclus, and Bateia. The city of Troy was most notably described as having broad streets, elegant, flourishing, well built, enclosed by great walls, and vastly rich in culture and goods.

Homer's Troy depicted a vast plain that led to the coast and a river that flowed across the plain into the coastal waters, the Scamander River. Troy set atop the plain with its tall walls and inside the walls a layout of rooms for the nobility to live and community to dwell. Schliemann's depiction is very accurate to Homer and if one looks at the scaled drawings he drew of the exterior wall and the interior rooms one can see how it would be hard to penetrate the well fortified citadel. The workings of many men brought the reality of Troy to life for all to see but this would not be the only evidence that these ancient and royal people lived.

Three men decided to find the existence of the Trojans by other means -- the form of writing tablets. Blegen, Evans, and Ventris were found during their time in the Aegean area tablets which they called Linear A and Linear B. These tablets were found at Pylos, Mycenae, Knossos, and Tiryns. They found an ancient form of writing on these tablets, one in stylized strokes in place of pictures called Linear A and one made up of characters in straight rows called Linear B. These men collected over a thousand tablets in all and the next step would be to decipher the language of archaic Greek. It was found through the aid of Ventris that the tablets were a list of inventories containing: lists of soldiers, slaves, servants, military lists and commanders, shepherds, livestock, and chariots used for military. Contained in these lists, to the excitement of its translators, were the names of extraordinary men of the time: Achilles, Hector, and Aeneas. Many of the trades mentioned on these tablets were also mentioned in Homer's "Iliad". Thus a painted picture has been established of the Trojans' descendants of Zarah (Zeus) by genealogy, a culture and plan of the city, and writing about all areas of life of the time. Homer's depiction of Troy some three hundred years after the Trojan War was a poem only in the sense of how he wrote about this great event. However, based on what facts are known, one can read it as an historical account of how it was seen through the eyes of a person living at that time.

The Greek author Homer took the legends of his ancestors with any other sources available to him and wrote the Iliad an epic poem in twenty-four poems dealing with the last year of the siege of Troy. Most authorities say the Iliad was written in the ninth or eighth century BC with a minority believing Homer composed his work at a later date. Homer's "Iliad" tells the story of how Achilles wins a battle with the prince Hector in the tenth year of the siege and that is where the poem ends with the burial rites given to him. A period of nine years of attacks on neighboring town by the Achaeans and Achilles had taken its toll on the Trojans and the final tenth year would be the beginning of the epic story of the "Iliad". The height of the epic battle between the Achaeans and the Trojans is death of Patroclus by Hector with the aid of Apollo. Achilles then decides, due to great grief for his longtime friend, to rejoin the battle to avenge his death. There was no man or god that could stop Achilles' rampage to the walls of Troy. Aeneas does battle with him to no avail, many princes of Troy battle to quell his fury. Aphrodite and the great Xanthus river god (Scammander) tried to subdue him but the rage of Achilles could not be held back now. He slays Hector, who is the last man to stand between him and the city walls and drags his body behind his chariot across the plain in front of the city showing his glory over the prince of Troy. Achilles decides to revel in his moment of glory by treating the body with disrespect and refuses to give it back. This would be the beginning of the end of the "Iliad" poems.

Zeus next seeks to subdue the insolence of Achilles by sending the god Hermes to escort King Priam, Hector's father and the ruler of Troy, into the Achaean camp. Priam tearfully pleads with Achilles to take pity on a father bereft of his son and return Hector's body. He invokes the memory of Achilles' own father Peleus. Achilles feels compassion for the aged king and returns the body of Hector, which is then taken to Troy. Both sides agree to a temporary truce and Hector receives a hero's funeral. Achilles further goes on to give Priam leave to hold a proper funeral for Hector complete with funeral games. He promises that no Greek will engage in combat for eleven days, but on the twelvth the war would resume. This is where the poems ends with tribute to Hector, a man of virture, strength, and courage who seeks no glory in battle but only to protect his family, his people, and his way of life. St. Augustine wrote about the two cities such as these sixteen hundred years later, of one man seeking glory for himself and one man seeking to do the will of his father Zarah (Zeus) and thus two cities are joined and later seperated.

The book of Virgil's "Aeneid" contains the best known account of the sack of Troy, which was besieged for ten years during the Trojan War. The fate foretold of many before the battle came to pass upon the Achaeans. Priam was brutally murdered by Achilles' son Neoptolemus (Pyrrhus) at the altar of Apollo along with one of his princely sons in the battle for Troy. Priam's reign ended in 1181 BC, after the tenth year of the First Trojan War, at the hands of their regional rivals. Achilles would die from a poison arrow (some say by the arrow and bow of Paris). Neoptolemus, Agememnon, and his elite army officers were slain by Orestes and his party out of outrage for his treatment by both. Thus, the justice of Zeus has found its way with the clearing away of the battlefield and the death of the Trojan rivals via its own people. This gave assurance to a new stage for the Trojans to once again regain what they had lost.

Helenus, a Trojan prince, son of Priam, fought bravely during the Trojan War and found himself in a most ambiguous position of aiding his enemy in order to be able to reclaim the city for the Trojans later. Neoptolemus captured Helenus when he retreated to Mount Ida during the Trojan War with his sister-in-law Andromache, who was the wife of slain Hector. They accompanied Neoptolemus (Pyrrhus) as captives to Epirus where Helenus persuaded him to settle. Helenus, meaning "of the light" had the gift of prophecy and was a seer for the royal family of Troy. Helenus gave an oracle when he was captured by the Greeks in the tenth year of the Trojan War by telling them that they would win the conflict only if the bones of Pelops were brought to Troy. And if the Palladium was taken from the city, Neoptolemus took the place of his father Achilles, and if Philoctetes was fetched to use the bow and arrows of Heracles that he had acquired from his father. This would be the second oracle given out by the seer Helenus, whose sister Cassandra was also a seer. The first oracle was given to his brother Hector in hopes of appeasing the gods and ending the war via divine intervention. Helenus in the story of Homer's the "Iliad" at one point tries to turn the tide of battle by employing his captain Hector and Aeneas to rally the troops from retreat to the walls of the city. He gives a plan to hold the troops where they stand until this is done while Hector must go back to the city and get their mother and all the noble women together. They then must visit the shrine of Athena to offer the royal of robes to her and lay by her knees. He also instructed him to sacrifice twelve heifers in her honor, all this to save the Trojans and hold back the man killing Diomedes. Hector would follow these plans by the seer but to no avail, as Athena had no plans for a Trojan victory.

The aspiration of seers or prophets has been thought to be that of judging the signs of what is yet to come. Their occupation is to read the signs of the gods, Apollo and Zeus, and foretell whether a man will meet death, disease, loss of property, and victory or defeat. They often interpreted the will of heaven by explaining dreams, watching the flights of birds, or watching the rustling of oak leaves. Their influence in some places was great and it has been said that priests were virtually the rulers of their regions. The magnitude of their undertakings allowed them to win high esteem and in some cases, like in Egypt, no king could rule without being a priest. Some say they were instruments of the gods and that the minds of the true seers, who are generally known as prophets, do not utter words by themselves but the gods speak through them. Those who may be thought as true seers have been compared with great poets, who compose not so much by wisdom and art but by nature and divine inspiration. Seers are inspired when they are enraptured and possessed by the gods and that is why they succeed in uttering true oracles of which they know nothing of what they say.

There are those who did not accept the divine nature of seers to be a decision making tool for men. One example is a bird in the sky that flew overhead of the Trojans causing Hector's comrades to persuade him not to attack. Hector responded to his fellow Trojan comrades with disdain for the alarm over their sighting. Hector and many other leaders believed that nothing could be done or known by either a layman or a seer if the gods do not wish it to be. This is their reason for finding it ridiculous to obey bad or good omens or in consulting the prophets whom they consider worthless. They would not in any way resort to divination, which they deemed to be just a way of making a living. They instead considered sound judgment and discernment as better means than the seer does. The unsurpassed method consists in addressing the gods directly by asking a blessing, while forgetting about divination, for whoever has the gods as friends does not need prophecy. This was Hector's stand on the matter of the seer as he is in the midst of war to protect his family and his city. He continues his stance by appealing to a higher form of divination by the father of the Trojans and the gods, in particular, the one who governs over both mortals and immortal, the counsel of Zeus.

Zeus did favor the Trojans but his grand plan would not be favorable to Hector or the city of Troy. Helenus' oracles would come true as sent down from Zeus, not in spite of the Trojan people but in the interest of them and the royal descent of his divine family. The four captains of the Trojans - Hector, Helenus, Aeneas, and Paris - found their fate in the will of Zeus.

All four would fight bravely for the people of Troy as they tried to make their way to the Achaean's ships to burn them and force the leaders to abandon their ambitions in favor of self-preservation of its army. Paris would flank the right with Aeneas to his left side and next to him Helenus who was flanked by the great prince Hector. Hector was a man of great strength and strategy who sought to join all the armored divisions of his allies in a disciplined manner and concentrated effort to drive the Achaeans from the coast. Although this was successful the gods were not in favor of the outcome and Patroclus would be sent into battle only to be slain by the spear of Hector. Hector then would be taken down in battle for the walls of Troy by Achilles' spear. The sign of the great prince was his last statements to his wife Andromache before going back out to battle after a brief rest. He told his wife he did not wish to leave her or his son and would prefer things to be different, but his duty to himself and to Troy was to go back to his army and finish a war he did not wish for.

The second captain and prince of Troy, Paris, was less honorable in his actions, yet did his duty for his city to prevent its destruction. Paris was considered the cause of the war in taking Helen from the shores of Sparta to Troy to be his wife. His bow and arrow would bring down many soldiers and his battle with Menelaus, although valiant to end the war before it got started, was a step backward in this regard. He would even foolishly leave the battle at one time to be with Helen, hoping that the gods would look favorable upon his actions. Paris' last known effort in the Trojan War was the death of Achilles by his poisoned arrow shot through his ankle in the Temple of Apollo were he sought to marry Polyxena. This would end the will of Zeus as set forth before the beginning of the Trojan War in its tenth year as the death of Achilles would follow shortly after he had achieved his glory.

Helenus was the third captain and prince of Troy and was formidable in battle as he was as a seer to the royal family of Troy. Helenus held his ground by Hector in the attempt to seize the Achaean's ships. A spear injured him to his hand causing his departure from battle. His subsequent capture at some point by Neoptolemus would begin a long journey to the Greek lands and then back to his homeland to rebuild the city as King of the Trojans.

Helenus was taken to Epirus with Andromache after their capture at Mount Ida. Epirus is an area on the west coastal waters of Greece where the oracle of Dodona is known to have been. Helenus was the founder of the cities of Buthrotum and Chaonia (from Trojan Chaon). The name Buthrotum is a word describing a place abounding with cattle and grazing land and was a perfect place for the new city. The ancient legend claims that having arrived at this site from Troy, Helenus sacrificed an ox to ensure his safe entry to Epirus. The wounded ox plunged into the sea, swam into a bay, and then walked onto a beach where it fell and died. Helenus took this as an omen and he called the place Buthrotos meaning "the wounded ox". According to Virgil's "Aeneid", Helenus was married to Andromache after the death of Neoptolemus by Orestes. Helenus married Andromache and became lord of the lands within Greece.

Helenus was now lord of Greece and King of the Trojans. He would have a son by Andromache named Genger (Zenter), a legendary Trojan king who would later have a son named Franko (Frankus). The citadel he built at Buthrotum Aeneas he would call a "little Troy" because it looked exactly like the citadel of Troy with its high walls and river nearby on the coast. Dodona was also in the region of Epirus and since Helenus was a seer it would not be far reaching to think he was part of the oracle to Zeus, with its rustling oak leaves. The last oracle given by Helenus would be to Aeneas, the last captain of the Trojans when they met after the Trojan War in Epirus.

The two Trojans that survived the war with the Achaeans, Helenus and Aeneas, were both from the line of Tros and Ilus, the founders of Troy and the Trojans. Their lineage breaks at the time of Laomedon. Helenus would be born to the King of Troy, Priam, and Aeneas would be born to Anchises and Aphrodite "goddess of love". Aeneas would fight gloriously and meet in battle against Achilles and fared better than any with the aid of the gods. Then when Hector is brought down they all would retreat to the walls of Troy and make a final decision on their next course of action. Aeneas decides to make a last attempt to save the city when awakened by a dream from Hector. The attempt to gather enough troops to take back the city was futile and thus Aeneas took his family and fled the city. He took his father Achises, his wife Creusa daughter of Priam, and his son named Ascanius (Lulus) just outside the wall of the city where many others had been gathered waiting orders from a high ranking member of the family. Aeneas' wife would not make it through the carnage as she was lost in the confusion of the moment. Aeneas attempted to search for her through the smoke, fire, and mist but could not find her so with the rest of his family he disembarked by ship to the safest land he could find. His family and followers would live a long hard journey from island to island before being swept ashore on Epirus where Andromache and Helenus had been living.

What transpired between Helenus and Aeneas on the shores of Epirus was a momentous occasion between two friends of the Trojans, deciding the future of two cities and empires. These two Trojan princes fought side by side with Hector and Paris in the front lines of the plains outside the city walls. Now they would meet arm in arm to decide the fate of the Trojan people.

When Aeneas' ship was swept to the shores of Epirus by the winds, Andromache was the first to meet him with answers and questions about the circumstances after the fall of Troy. Then Helenus with great joy for his friend came down from the slimmed down version of Troy and met him with open arms, food, and drink. A few days passed and then as s sailing wind came a departure was of necessity, but before Aeneas left he asked the seer for s divine path to sail by. Then with the aid of Apollo and ceremonial rites given, he spoke of the path he should take, which would lead him to a great place to build his high city walls in Italy. Then Aeneas spoke a final word before setting sail, that when his city in Hesperia is built, that they both could look back to their founder Dardanus and their heirs would make a single Troy. Thus the Trojan line split, with one settling in what would become Rome and the other back to the lands of Troy. Both cities would face hardships and also prosper before meeting again in what would become Europe in the upper Rhine region.

The Trojan royal family was restored to power during the second Trojan War in 1149 BC. The descendants of Helenus regained control of Troy from the Greeks and restored the Royal House of Dardanus to the city. The Spanish historian Bartholome Gutierrez records the names of Helenus' descendants who controlled Troy and the surrounding region until the Third Trojan War in 677 BC. The royal lineage continued from Genger (Zenter) to Basabiliano II, who were all kings of the Trojans and Troy. Alexander (second Paris) was the last generation in Troy when the third Trojan War occurred. The population fled to the northern shores of the Black Sea in what is Eastern Europe. In all about 12,000 Trojans fled by ship to the land at the mouth of the Tanais and from there they moved to Pannonia near the Danube and Macedonia over a period of 234 years up to 445 B.C. It was not until this time that a new king was established among the refugees of Troy in Southeastern Europe by the name of Antenor I a Cimmerian. The Cimmerians were of the Thracian region living around the Black Sea. Their migration did not end here; the Trojan Phrygians moved further into Europe to the mouth of the Rhine where they built a new Troy at Xanten (river named after Xanthus in Phrygia). The Romans called this new city Troia Nova. There in the region of Scynthia Minor they settled for a number of years until a series of wars began with the Goths for Scandinavia, where King Antenor I would fall in battle.

The area settled was the ancient territory of the German Cimbri and thus they are Sicambri, and Marcomirus I would become their new king. A prophecy was given to him by a priest to go west and victories would follow over the Gauls and Roman legions. An embassy was sent to the German Saxon asking for land to settle. They moved northwest from the Danube to the Rhine with half a million warriors and civilians. He then conquered all of Gaul making a brother governor while another brother moved into what was called West Friesland. This was the first major victory that was prophecy to Marcomirus I. His son Antenor II married Cambra, the daughter of King Belinus of Britain. She introduced to the priests and priestesses the worship of Jupiter (Zeus) at an area of the mouth of the river Rhine. The populace worshipped other gods as well including Pallas Athena. The king built a new temple in honor of Zeus for the descendants of the Trojans from Troy after 260 years and fourteen generations of migration westward.

The Sicambris used harsh tactics to win their battles against the Gauls and Goths including combining their army with the Saxons inflicting heavy casualties amongst the enemy. One failed assault by the Gauls against the officers of the Sicambri left nearly a hundred thousand lives lost. There was an intense internal pressure on the leaders to produce victories in any way possible in order to establish a stronghold and dominance in the area. Each leader kept the priests and priestesses in high regard while at the same time maneuvering the army and building forts against Gaulish incursions, as did Bassanus who spent much of his time on this. He built the city of Bassanburg (called Aix la Chaepelle by Trithemius). He took over the duties of priest at the site of Jupiter where the prophets flourished in his time. He was also very successful against the Saxons and won a great victory at Westphalians. The foothold in the Rhine was beginning to emanate outwards.

Nicanor, the grandson of Bassanus, was also very successful in combining the military to defeat the Goths. He also aided his father in law the king of Britain, whose daughter, Constantina, he married to defeat the Orcades and Orkneys. The marriages between the Britains and the Sicambri were very significant in regards to religion and to the power struggle within the area. The Roman legion would begin to be the next opposition faced by the Sicambri in 200 BC and up to 41 BC. The last battle fought by a Sicambri king was Antharius who battled against the army of Ceasar. There was no winner of this battle but the Gauls entered the battle against him and he was slain. His son was named Francus, as was Helenus of

Troy's grandson. This would begin the age of the Franks who would transform the continent and its population over the next thousand years.

The fall of Troy created a migration by a great race that was determined to continue their traditions as set forth by their forefathers. A citadel now existed in some form in Troy of the Aegean, Epirus of Greece, Rome in Italy, and Xanten in the Rhine of upper Europe. All these were situated on a coastal water area facing the sea with a great plain in front of the citadel. The high wall and the plain in front were meant to be a great defense against enemies. It allowed them to see a great distance out to the sea to mark their enemies before arriving on land. Once on the land the enemy had to march quite a distance before reaching the great wall, which was virtually impenetrable. The backside of the citadel was open to the land behind it occupied by many different inhabitants and used for trade and allies in their battles. These where the tactics used by the Trojans which allowed them to survive many battles. The will of God thus had been done as was handed down when it was said:

> *"Judah, thy brethren shall praise thee: thy hands shall be on the back of thine enemy; thy father's children shall adore thee. Judah is a lion's whelp: from the sprouting, my son, thou art gone up: lying down, thou hast slept as a lion, and as a lion's whelp; who shall awake him? A prince shall not be lacking out of Judah, and a leader from his thighs, until the things come that are laid up for him; and He shall be the expectation of the nations."*

Many nations were now centered on this blessing, from the Mediterranean to Europe. The will of Zeus had also come to pass as the population followed his teachings through the oracles set up in different locations as they migrated westward. Finally, justice had come to aid those and delivered them from their enemies. Repeatedly justice would follow upon the virtuous and righteous people that did the will of Zeus. To remind the populace of this they built their temple to Jupiter at the mouth of the Rine.

III

MEROVINGIAN DYNASTY
FRANKS

Bow your head in meekness, Sicamber. Worship what you have
burnt, burn what you have been won't to worship.

Bishop Remigius of Rheims, LH II. 31, Gregory of Tours

THE AGE OF THE Franks began a tremendous struggle amongst the existing
inhabitants of the Upper Rhine region they settled in and the survival of the
royal family lineage and their ancestral doctrine. The Franks survived by
adopting the military prowess and tactics of their ancestors. By staying within
the ancestral doctrine, allying during times of battle with their neighbors and
evolving at the same time to higher ideas intellectually and spiritually they
were able to overcome their enemies. They consolidated the neighboring tribes
under their laws. The precedence of the Franks that was initially adopted by
Clovis the Great, King of all the Franks, was Christianity. Acceptance of
this religion gave the Franks a higher standing amongst neighboring tribes,
throughout their populace, and the Papal States. The Franks were always in
the forefront to the changes that needed to be made to become the kings and
later emperors of the populace within their continental region, which became
an empire based on Christianity.

The Franks derived their name from Frankus. He lived in 41 BC– 13 AD,
and led the battles against the Goths and Gauls with significant victories and
thus the Sicambri (Trojan) changed their name by edict of the people's request.
Frankus allied his population with the Germans and the Saxons to defeat the
Roman army that governed and occupied the region. The appearance and
recognition of the Franks would not happen until much later time when
military generals of his descendants won battles over the Romans.

The Franks would begin as a tribe that would pick its leaders based on
their skill and courage in battle. They were a hereditary monarchy chosen

for the duration of battles against the enemy at a particular time. They were known as a "free" and "fierce" people among the Germans they lived with. Loyalty was given to the tribe and not to the loose confederation with the Germans they settled with. Thus, to be called a Frank had to do with two things, the area you lived in (Gaul, Friesland, Upper Rhine) and your political alliance with the leader of the tribe, who would later become king. But not necessarily your ethnicity.

The idea that the Franks came from the descendants of the Trojans has been substantiated by historical facts. The first of these is the genealogy that has been collected by several sources including the previously named Spanish historian Bartholome Gutierrez. The Roman governing body and military when engaged in battle also documented the western movement of the Trojans. The similarities in traditions between the early Franks and Trojans in religion (Temples to Jupiter, Zeus), burial rites (personal effects, armor, and horses), military expertise, and names used (Xanten, Frankus, Antenor) give credence to their royal and tribal connections. Based on these facts the Trojans can be connected to the Franks from the Merovingian Dynasty, Arnulfian Dynasty, and Carolingian Dynasty of which a central royal family continuously led them through battles and religious changes. The Frankish royal family was expected to lead the tribe with courage and bravery and to unite the populace under a central governing body. These Franks continued an upward evolution within their royal family while at the same time increasing the outward control over territory. The names within this royal family are Frankus, a king of the Franconians, Childeric I, king of the Franks, Clovis, Christian king of all the Franks, Brunhilda, Frankish Queen, Pepin, Mayor of the Palace, and Charlemagne, king of the Franks and Holy Roman Emperor.

The distinguishing characteristics of the Franks was to evolve from what was considered a barbarian race to a strong, generously looking, high moral stature, and warm regard for culture. It did not degenerate as did the Roman Empire before it but sprang from its youth of the Merovingian Dynasty to the Carolingian Dynasty of Charlemagne. This transformation would begin with Marcomir IV when he married Athilde "Princess of Britain" somewhere between 125 – 146 A.D. She was the daughter of King Coel (Coilus) in the line of descendancy of Pharah twin of Zarah which King David and Joseph of Arimathea would come from. The brother line of the scarlet thread united and continued to hold and preserve the scepter of Judah. The scepter shall not depart from Judah as one from these lines will always wear the crown. Then at some future time, there will be a gathering of the people and the breaches of the past healed. The families of the Frankish leader and the Princess would produce four "Great" rulers – Constantine the Great, Clovis the Great,

Charles the Great "Charlemagne", and Alfred the Great. These rulers all had similar traits in religious beliefs, laws, military abilities, governing, and mercy upon their enemy. But before every great king and great society there is a great general that precedes them and this would be the case before Clovis came to become the King of All the Franks.

Generals that battled with the Romans and rose to great esteem for their military abilities were Sunno, Pharamond, Chlodion, and Merowich (Merowig) starting the Merovingian Dynasty around 289 A.D. The names mentioned were not kings but during this period considered by what Gregory of Tours, historian of the Frankish people, called Gennobaudes "leaders". They fought battles alongside other tribes already established in the area before they arrived namely the Chamavi, Bruceri, Chattuari, Salians, Amsivarii, Tubantes, Frisians, and Chauci in attacks across the Rhine to disrupt the Roman army with raids. One of the main battles fought by Pharamond, Duke of the Franks, was in Cologne in 356 in an attempt to cross the Rhine river and move westward. Julian retook Cologne and drove back the Frankish alliance upon which they settled with the Roman Empire until the mid-fifth century. Clodio would win great success in his battles but then finally lost in battle against Aetius, the Roman commander of Gaul. He regrouped and took all the country as far as the Somme River and making Tournai the capital of the Franks.

The line of Clodio would split into two lines leading to the Merovingian Dynasty and Merowig and the other leading to the Arnulfian and Carolingian Dynasties of Pepin and Charlemagne. Merowig and his son Childeric I were of the Salian Franks to the east of the Rhine. They sought to gain common ground with the Romans while at the same time defeating their enemies to the north and northeast of them. Merowig is only known by stories of Gregory of Tours who establishes him as a king of the Salian region who won many battles. His success led to the creation of a Dynasty of Franks who could not be defeated. Childeric I his son would continue this by winning over the Romans and received lands from them as a "foederatus". He fought alongside the Romans in battle, creating honor for him in their military fostering a mutual respect between the Romans and the Franks. From here the line of generals ends and the line of kings established by Clovis, Christian king of all the Franks, begins.

Facts about Childeric I are more plentiful than any other Frankish King due to the grave found in the Church of Saint Brice in Tournai. The most interesting of the items found were gold bees and a ring with the inscription 'Childerici Regis'. He is known for his battle at Orleans and for establishing a capital at Tournai. Campaigns in Angers, Paris and Burgundy by Childeric I would help consolidate his son's efforts in the future.

When Clovis came to be king of the Franks the Roman Empire had withdrawn from most of Europe to Constantinople, which would be called the Byzantine Empire. The emperor was still in control of the Papal States and had his say in the day to day business of them. However, with the change in the capital of the empire, over time there was less control in this concern. As the Frankish Empire grew and the need for a substitute patrician for the Pope increased for localized support the window of power slowly opened for the Frankish king. First there would be a consolidation of power within the Frankish kingdom and recognition of it along with acceptance of Christianity before this transpired.

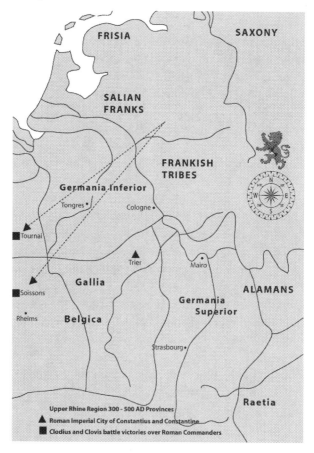

Clovis found it necessary to bring all the tribes of the Franks under one king and one religion. He did this by showing that Christianity was righteous in that it would strengthen and make prosperous the Franks. Then he won over the populace of neighboring kings and brought them into the Frankish realm. By doing these two things, it was significantly easier to triumph over armies larger than his. The army Clovis gathered gained the Franks more lands given over to the bishops. A beginning of nationality introduced many rewards from this institution. When Clovis came to be king of the Salian Franks he inherited an area of what is today Belgium and northwestern Gaul. His army numbered only a few thousand well-coordinated and agile men with a reputation for accomplishing the impossible. Rivals of his time were the Burgundians (Patricians of the Pope under Gundobad), Visgoths, and Soissons under Roman occupation. Victories came quickly to the king who succeeded at the age of sixteen. Soissons under the rule of Syagrius, a collaborator with his father in the past, would be the first military directive of Clovis and then his army would move against the Alamans. This battle of Zulpich did not go well for the King of the Franks until he decided to call upon Christ in a prayer. Clovis decided to give his word that if the battle was won he would convert and truly submit to Christianity by baptism, upon which he divinely did. This would be the first step toward the conversion to Christianity by the Franks and this King of all Franks.

The reason for the willingness to move towards the acceptance of Christianity came during the time of Clovis. The Frankish King had wished to move southward after these victories in localized areas of the north. Burgundy stood between him and the Papal states. Burgundy's leader was Gundobad who was a Christian king but held views not accepted by the church. Remy of Rheims was a Catholic bishop in the court used for the education of the royal household. The bishop had contacts also within the royal household of the Franks, counterparts to the Burgundians. The church agreed to combine the two regions through marriage and thus strengthen the church. A plan was set to have Clovis marry the strong minded and pretty princess, Clotild. The combination of the Catholic faith and a strong leader was of great advantage to the church and they thought highly of both in this regard. Gundobad, fearing the upheaval he did not wish in the Burgundians, had her father and family slain and sparing her life only. Now there would be a reason to come to the aid of the Catholic Church and Burgundy.

The Catholic Church supported the idea of Remy of Rheims for a romance that would solidify the church and populace under Clovis. Clovis sent emissaries to pay alms to the princess Clotild who received them like a true Christian. A message was given to Clovis upon their return of the princess' great beauty. Clovis asked for her hand in marriage and Gundobad gave way in respect for the Frankish King. Clothild left on horseback in a hurried manner with escorts towards the Frankish court but Gundobad had a change of mind. A Burgundian regiment set out to bring the princess back but retrieved only the treasure after repulsion by the escort.

Clotild wished that her sons and daughters be baptized into the Catholic faith. Her first son was but did not live, which outraged the Frankish King Clovis. Then another son was born and baptized, but while ailing, a prayer helped him live through it. Thus three signs to Clovis changed him over to Christianity: victory in battle, marriage to a Catholic princess, and the birth and baptism of his son.

Clovis held to his agreement for baptism along with a few thousand of his soldiers who were in battle at Soissons. Conversion had its disadvantages as part of his army went over to the rivals and many adversaries who were amongst the Franks, but Clovis had a comprehension of future events and thus these issues did not cause him concern. The king held a vast clergy with bishops that the populace were slowly accepting and he had won great victories for his people. The baptism took place in Rheims by the bishop Remy on Christmas day 503. The sacrament was made into something that was magnificent as the church was decorated and adorned with linens and candles; it was a delight to all who were there. Then the bishop pronounced to the Sicamber (in reference to his ancestors of the Sicambri) to worship what he would have burned and to burn what he had been worshipping. This is probably in reference to the gods his ancestors had worshipped and the idols they prayed to including Jupiter (Zeus) and Juno (Hera). Thus the conversion of Clovis had become the passing away by the royal line of one great will and the cornerstone to the next great will of Christianity.

The oracles from 587 BC to 700 AD went into decline and later would be restored many times over until they finally were distinguished. A great change had taken place in regards to the oracles even before Clovis time by Constantine the Great who prohibited them, punishable by death, during his reformation acts and tendency to aid the Catholic faith within the Roman Empire. This would, however, again be overturned by Emperor Julian who sought out consultation at Dodona. The oracles were again banned by Theodosius in 385 AD and after centuries of battles by the Romans much destruction was caused to all the oracle buildings. The populace's acceptance of Christianity in their place brought them into disuse. Popular public demand for the new Christian faith would now take their place as the precedence of the new age.

Acceptance of Christianity has three stages upon which must be completed for full conversion to be realized. The stages are intellectual acceptance of Christ's message, to bring the message forth to followers, and the ceremony of baptism and membership in the community of Christians. Clovis' became the first king to advance through all three stages of acceptance while overcoming the pagan traditions of his Frankish tribal ancestry. This process would be followed by all succeeding kings of the Franks and by all kings within this royal lineage. This king would bring it forth to his fellow people; the next great king would bring it forth to an empire, and the succeeding ones to an international level.

Clovis would now turn his attention to his uncle Gundobad, who had murdered Clotild's parents before they were married. Gundobad was disposed for a time period with the aid of his brother and then regained his leadership and alliance with the Franks to help in the upcoming battles with the Visgoths. Clovis' army passed by St. Martin and St. Hilary of Poitiers as they engaged the Visgoths, upon which their leader Alaric II was killed with many Gallo-Roman senators. This would almost double the territory under the Franks in Gaul, a highly rich region under Roman leadership. The Franks took over whatever Roman administration was left in the region. Upon hearing of this Emperor Anastasius sent Clovis a letter from Constantinople in recognition of his success and granting him full sanction as consul. A grand celebration followed at St. Martin in honor of his great victory for the Frankish kingdom. This victory had given Clovis a basis to become ruler of the Romans and to extend his power over larger regions. The king of the Franks and consul would now make his residence at the city of Paris due to its central location in the kingdom.

The recognition by the Roman Emperor Anastasius to Clovis king of the Franks could be seen as a resolution of the oracle from Helenus to Aeneas when they met in Epirus. As mentioned earlier, there they met as equals and friends both with different journeys ahead of them, and Helenus stated that one day the two cities which were once of Dardanus would meet again. The last oracle of Zeus was revealed with the passing of traditions upon which his will had stood for centuries. In 511 Clovis died in Paris and was buried in the Church of Saint Peter and Saint Paul which he and Clotild had built. Clovis had ended his reign and would be known for developing the region of what is modern day France (*Francia*).

An independent kingdom of Burgundy would come under the rule of the sons of the Frankish king. This would continue until the Arnulfians and Carolingians came to power based on their great strength and saintly status. They were of the same Frankish descent but had more of a monarchist and religious attitude than did their closest ancestors. This line of royal Franks did not believe in absolutism of a certain Frankish Queen Brunhilda, who had married Siegbert I, and thus fought to distinguish its idea. The church and its clergy were, until that time passed, a basis for strengthening their position.

The Merovingian Dynasty lasted from about 430 to 721 with the royal family of the Franks ruling as kings in all aspects in order to increase its populace and strength in a region that was occupied by many different tribes as well as the Romans. Their military victories can be attributed to the practice of choosing as king the strongest and most successful members of their tribe.

The unity of the Franks under the king could be attributed to bringing a common cause to the populace. This was achieved by instituting the fact that survival of the tribe brought prosperity and lands, while acceptance of Christianity brought with it allegiances to defend against rivals. Both were used to strengthen the core of the Frankish kingdom while at the same time increasing its stronghold further outward over time. An example of this is Charibert I a grandson of Clovis who was ruler over many areas of the Frankish kingdom including the lands between the Somme and the Loire with Paris as the capital. This region included Rouen, Tours, Aquitaine, Novempopulana, Poitiers, Limoges, Bordeaux, Toulouse, Cahors, and Albi. His daughter Bertha married the king of Kent, a pagan, around 590. This marriage allowed for the arrival of Augustine's mission in 597. This Christian mission was allowed to stay in Canterbury while practicing the conversions first in Kent and then later of the Anglo-Saxons. Thus, Christianity played a major role in the lives of the populace and in the strategic affairs of the Frankish kings.

Grandsons of Clovis would seek to continue his acceptance and spread of Christianity. But their hopes of this would be lessened due to the fact that they were caught up in a family struggle between four brothers and the division of Clovis' gains in Gaul and Germany. The kingdom would be broken up into four shares between Chilperic I, Charibert, Guntram, and Segibert I in the corresponding regions of Paris, Orleans, Neustria, and Austrasia. The lands of Charibert as mentioned earlier were gained from his uncle Childebert I, son of Clovis. Guntram's lands would be that of Orleans and Burgundy all the way to the Alps from his uncle Chlodomir also the son of Clovis. Then Chilperic I gained the lands of Neustria and Soissons, the kingdom to the west, which came from his father Theudebald son of Clovis. The last lot drawn of the lands of Clovis was Segibert I by his father Chlothar I who would own Austrasia, which was a region from Northeast Gaul, Germany and the Saxon lands. They each swore an oath by the saints not to encroach on one another's lands and to respect the lots drawn. The nature of the Franks made this a weak alliance for there is naturally only one king who is the strongest of them all; accordingly, this would not be upheld for any length of time.

During Segibert I's campaigns into the Rhine in Germany there would be an encroachment onto other lands. In so doing Chilperic took it upon himself to take Rheims but he was countered by his brother and lost the capital of Neustria, Soissons. This would be the beginning of altercations between each of the brothers, which would continue until only one could be crowned king of the kingdom of all four lands.

The next two main events would pit the same two brothers against each other while Guntram would play peacemaker between them. The death of

Charibert left his treasures to Guntram in 567. Chilperic was considering marrying Galswinth, the sister of Brunhilda and wife of Segibert I. An unfortunate event occurred when Galswinth was murdered, supposedly by Chilperic, causing a great uprising by Brunhilda. She wanted her husband to attack his brother in an act of justice. However, Guntram sought to dissuade Segibert I from such an act and instead decided the law of the Franks should resolve the conflict and bring justice to those guilty of any act of wrongdoing. When final judgment came down from the Council, Chilperic was found guilty. This did not end the struggle between the two Frankish Kings but only subsided it for a time until one or the other could decide their next step in bringing the lands of the other into their own kingdom.

Chilperic sought to engage quickly upon Segibert I in reprisals while he was away in remote areas of his kingdom. He sent his son Clovis to Tours and Poitiers where he came into the cities unopposed by the military. This maneuver allowed him to be in a good position to take back the lands he gave up under the judicial system of the Franks. Segibert I took action against this by sending one of his top generals, Mummolus, to Tours to defeat Clovis. Chilperic's son sought refuge from this most distinguished general in Poitiers. Mummolus had the counts and bishops assemble the peoples, both Roman and Frank, at Tours to swear an allegiance to Segibert I. The general, who was the greatest tactician during this period, next attacked Clovis in Poitiers. He won without much resistance from the army that had gathered in defense of the city. The two cities taken by Chilperic and his son were now back in the hands of Segibert I, who was given allegiance by all as king of the kingdom.

These events did not diminish Chilperic's desire to acquire the lands handed over to Brunhilda. His next step was full devastation of the lands given up to her and Sigebert I. A campaign was introduced to lay waste to all that was put in order by his grandfather Clovis, including churches, houses, convents and the homes throughout the countryside. To this act of devastation during the year 574, Segibert found only one response by gathering all the armored divisions within his kingdom and beyond to march against the divisions of his brother. Chilperic sought to retreat and find a favorable position in which to attack or gain peace terms. Chilperic decided on the latter and gave back the cities that belonged to his brother, including Tours and Poitier, with full acknowledgment of the terms drawn up during the initial dividing of Clovis' lands. Segibert I did not stop here and went to Paris to consolidate his wins for future reprisals. Now he would begin moving about the kingdom taking in all the cities while Chilperic sought refuge with his wife and children in Tournai. Since the struggles between the two Frankish kings seemed to be settled, Brunhilda left to meet her husband in

Paris in grand style consisting of a baggage train full on golden ornaments and jewels.

It was not only Guntram who sought to bring peace back to all the kingdoms and the three brothers but also Bishop Germanus (St. Germain). The bishop implored both sides to come to terms in a most Christian way and to turn away from the barbarian way of the past. His efforts would leave him in a state of ill health from the insistent manner of battles between the two Frankish kings. Segibert I left Paris for Tournai to seek out his brother in arms. On the outskirts of Tournai a site was set up in Vitry sur la Scarpe as a meeting place for the ceremony of the crown of the Western Frank King Segibert I. The royal inauguration was a splendid occasion in the Frankish style, and at the end came festivities in the form of banquets with combat between the soldiers. During these festivities two men arrived from the camp of Chilperic with a mission to murder the new Frankish king before his reign could begin. Segibert I accepted the men as any Frank would and upon bidding them audience in his tent they stabbed him several times before both being subdued and killed in return. Thus the message given by St. Germain transpired and the brother seeking to be overly just to the brother who had wronged the other found only death awaiting him as he left for Tournai. St. Germain believed the non-Christian way of the two brothers led to the divine end that brought only misery to the kingdom and the royal household.

There was now for the first time of the age of the Franks a Queen at the head of the royal household over Neustria. She resided in Paris until deciding her next move against Chilperic's ambitious nature. She sent her son Childebert II to Metz in a most secret way. There he would be more than welcomed by the Franks, who were more than ready to set up a new King of the Franks in Austrasia. At the age of five he was proclaimed king by the bishops and lords to rule over the kingdom of the Franks. Chilperic and his son Merovech, who found her to be a most enchanting Queen, placed Brunhilda under guard at Paris during this time. She left for Rouen being unharmed by Chilperic's guards and sometime after her arrival married Merovech without the consent of Chilperic. The rise of Queen Brunhilda and her son Childerbert II would bring a new age of Absolutism to the Franks with the consolidation of the lands of the kingdom. It would be until the Arnulfian Dynasty that the fall of this style of government would change under Pepin and the more saintly and generous Franks. The age of destruction and strife, however, were behind the Franks, allowing them to concentrate on their devotion to the Christian faith.

The church played a major part in both the populace and government levels of society during the Merovingian Dynasty. Archbishops as well as priests dealt with the everyday lay person while the educated bishops were handling the administrative dealings of the day. The most influential member of the Christian church during the early Frankish times was St. Denis. The Bishop of France was sent to the Frankish kingdom in Gaul around the third century as told by Gregory of Tours. He was of high esteem within the church during this time due to being the first convert of St. Paul. St. Denis' ability to increase the awareness of the church made him the most prominent saints of France. The assignment given to St. Denis was the area that would be known as Paris. He would become the first bishop of the city and performed miracles and wonders under persecution by the Romans. He became a martyr when he was beheaded on the highest hill in Paris. Afterwards he picked up his head singing a sermon all the way to a place which would be the Saint Denis Basilica, a burial place for the kings of France.

Many monasteries and churches were built during Frankish times. Some were for the sole purpose of a given family who appointed their own family members to positions in them. An estimate around 13 churches in Tours and over 4,000 within the kingdom of Gaul had been established by 600 A.D. As mentioned before, families built monasteries, as did the monarchs themselves such as Clovis who built the church of the Holy Apostles in Paris and St. Martin in Autun. Childebert I built the church of the Holy Cross and St. Vincent in Paris as well as St. Stephen. These churches of the time were small but grand in design and signified the power invested in them through the church and God. The churches to some degree were used to mark the Frankish kingdom's territory for as it grew outward so did the building of churches to its farthest most perimeter. An attack on a church was considered an attack on the royal family and king of the Franks. Churches were also built in rival territory to gain footholds through possible conversions. The building of churches was as instrumental as military victories during the age of the Merovingian Dynasty.

Frankish kings would have duties performed for them in both church and military related areas by bishops, counts, and dukes who were considered part of the royal family. Kings were above the church and made summons of bishops to point out what decisions were needed and to hand down punishment to those who did not follow in a lawful or holy way in their duties. Church councils were a way for the king to know what was happening throughout the kingdom and were made up of bishops, clerics, and local aristocrats. The bishops would also aid in sending the word of the king out to the dioceses and to hand down judgment as well as create peace in the kingdom.

The official in charge of watching the bishops, holding law court and tax collection was the count (grafio) who also in turn was watched by the bishop. Some counts were given the duties of both civil and military affairs for their given province. Dukes were also officials that had the same duties as counts and each were of equal status with the formal title of patricius (patronage to the king) expected to keep up the revenue in the royal treasury. The king had at his disposal many patricius to perform necessary duties throughout the Frankish kingdom. The Frankish King had a court of religious clerics and the bishops to aid him in church and civil affairs. The count and duke handed down laws and military affairs in their province to safeguard the kingdom as well as engage in campaigns against rivals and enemies of Christianity. These positions were appointed and could be taken away without hesitancy upon wrong action concerning the king and kingdom.

What Clovis had done for the Franks during his kingship would be indoctrinated by a descendant of his seven generations later in Wessex in an area of the southern region of what is now England. Egbert was in fact strongly attached to the Frankish Kingdom in more than one way. Expelled for thirteen years by the reigning king, he sought to gain knowledge in the Frankish system of government and customs. There he was married to the Frankish Princess Redburga, possible sister in law to Charlemagne, and since living at the time of Charlemagne there is some chance that he came in contact with his ideas for the administration of a successful kingdom. This clearly is shown when he returned to the British Isles and won victories in West Welsh, Cornwall, Mercia, Kent, Surrey, Sussex , Essex, and to some extent over the Danes. His descendant and successor King of England would be Alfred the Great who later came to struggle against the Danes as well. Another kingdom was being established under the guise of the Franks and Christianity would be brought with them.

The Franks had been very prosperous under the Merovingian kings through the military victories and prestige obtained by the acceptance of Christianity. However, the success of the Franks would be based on the continuation of these military victories outward from the kingdom as well as a firm establishment of their unity with the Papal States, along with the Popes' blessing for their causes. The saintly status that would rise amongst the descendants and the promise for military protection for the Pope would solidify their needs for growth, which would become an empire.

IV

ARNULFIAN
AND
CAROLINGIAN DYNASTY
FRANKS

The King, who excelled all the princes of his time in wisdom and
greatness of soul, did not suffer difficulty to deter him or danger
to daunt him from anything that had to be taken up or carried
through, for he had trained himself to bear and endure whatever
came, without yielding in adversity, or trusting to the deceitful
favors of fortune in prosperity.

Life of Charlemagne, Einhard 30

THE SUPREME AGE OF the Franks would rise from what had been achieved by
the first great leader Clovis during the Merovingian Dynasty. The Frankish
king's descendants would attain saintly status and Holy Roman Emperor,
which would be attained by the will of the people, the royal family of the
Franks, the Pope, and God. The timeline of success would be set forth by
the Franks as follows: win small victories with their allies, demonstrate their
military might against the Romans, unite the populace through the Christian
faith, extend their power by military and alliances, be recognized by the
Papal States, gain higher standing within the church, win victories for the
people and the church, become protectorate of the Pope and Emperor of the
Christian faith. Charlemagne, Charles the Great, would bring a golden age
to the Western civilization and the Western Empire. The ability to unify the
church and the state would become one of the most momentous historical
achievements known to the European continent. Charlemagne was a man
of great strength and virtue who could orchestrate both his military might
as well as his enduring faith in God to create an Empire that would be the

symbol to all leaders and nations to follow. What he and his forefathers achieved would not be lost but only reshaped due to the evolving ideas adopted by each generation.

Clovis descendants would begin reconstruction at the governmental level as well as the kingship. Land acquisition had brought many riches upon the kingdom and a larger populace to govern. A need for more control over kingship would move toward a reconstruction of governing and also would solve the issue of the prosperity that was being created. A cessation of the old practice of assemblies of warriors was instituted. These assemblies would be a counsel to the king and he would make decisions on them based on their military successes. Thus the kings did away with these assemblies to consolidate their power over the realms. A new governing body was put in place, a council made up of generals, provincial dignitaries (counts and dukes), bishops, and courtiers. The presiding member of the council or royal cabinet was the Mayor of the Palace and became an influential figure within the kingdom.

The position of Mayor of the Palace was given to the highest military warrior with statesman like qualities. His duties included administrative and domestic duties as well as defending the king against contests by the aristocracy. The Mayor of the Palace in times where the king was too young to rule would become an executor with royal powers. The official holding this position would change hands many times due to their quick rise to power over time and would later become the resurgence of disputes between Austrasia and Neustria-Burgundy.

Pepin the Younger of Austrasian aristocracy would emerge to put down what was then thought of as the Neustrian tyrant. He was the grandson of Arnulf, Bishop of Betz a Saint of his time as was his mother Begga a daughter of Pepin the Old. Begga was a Saint with virtuous qualities who had a devotion to her family as well as religious affairs. Pepin the Younger would also become a Saint, although never formally canonized, who accepted his followers' loyalty but not under fear. His agenda was to create unity and hope through his patience and wisdom that he had inherited from his mother Begga. Pepin sought peaceful negotiations between the Neustrian Mayor of the Palace, but was turned away and in so doing defeated them in a military battle.

Pepin became the central authority and Mayor of the Palace ending the Merovingian Dynasty and creating after two more generations a new dynasty of saintly kings, called the Arnulfian Dynasty. Austrasia, Neustria, and Burgundy were now under the administration of the House of Pepin and the Mayor of the Palace. Boundaries of old were restored to the Frankish kingdom and enemies such as the Saxons were once again put down in awe of the new consolidation. This would pave the way for the next generations that would follow in creating an Empire in the west replacing the Roman Empire that had existed for so long in the region. Pepin brought forth a new proposition for his enemies of being merciful and under conditions of peace they would accept Christianity. Many of the rivals to the Frankish kingdom would accept these terms as gratitude for mercy in battle, however there would be others, mainly the Saxons, who would be more difficult to subdue.

Another rival entering from Spain would emerge calling for the need of the Christian Franks to have a strong military leader to serve the duties of the people and the church. Charles Martel had created the first standing army of his time since the Romans needed in upcoming battles. The Moslem army had entered into the Frankish kingdom and into Burgundy, destroying cities there. Charles Martel was now Mayor of the Palace and was holding his northern border while this invasion was occurring. He made the decision to confront the enemy with a small regiment in a defensive position. Before the cavalry could breakthrough the lines they went on the offensive, destroyed the Moslem army, and killed their leader. For this great victory in what would be called the "Battle of Tours", Charles Martel was hence called "The Hammer" due to the defeat against a much larger force in battle. Employed in this battle were great military ideas such as armored mounted soldiers with long lances to drive back the invading army. Charles Martel was the Christian savior of what would be known as Europe, and looked upon by the Pope as a possible defender of the spiritual empire. The unification of Frankish Gaul would give his sons the necessary leverage to consolidate their power and aid the Pope against his rivals. His son Pepin would become Mayor of Neustria and Burgundy while Carolman Mayor of Austrasia.

Charles Martel and his sons were in agreement that there was a need for reform in Frankish Gauland supported the work of Archbishop Boniface. The main missionary was in Germany and that is where Boniface baptized and destroyed idolatry figures in the region. He organized the bishops in the area and founded monasteries for the populaces. He believed in the supreme authority of Rome allying himself with the Franks. The Pope made him archbishop of Mainz in the Frankish kingdom, which would become his secular ally as well. Boniface was allowed to adopt laws for the clergy of the church and to change the king's ability to use money from the church for military purposes along with the land and buildings they owned. A joining of church and state would be made, and also between the Franks and the Pope with the catalyst being Boniface. Pepin was anointed king of the Franks by the archbishop with the backing of his clergy and the Frankish church.

The crowning of Pepin as king of the Franks was not the guarantee that was needed to retain the royal position over the next generations. An alliance was needed with the Pope for even greater strength to rule over the kingdom.

The Lombards under Aistulf marched on Rome and Pope Stephen in 753, which would bring cause to ask the Frankish king for protection since the appeals to the Emperor of Constantinople for protection were in vain.

A great legend would then begin from here when Pope Stephen II traveled through the Alps with its bad climates and great heights in 754 to Burgundy to meet Pepin for re-crowning under the Papal authority. The Papal visit was the first by a Pope to Gaul especially in bad weather. Charlemagne his son would be there to meet the Pope to escort him to the monastery at St. Denis. This meeting in the woods would be the entry into a future meeting in Rome that would change Europe for centuries to come. The Roman title of Patricius was given to Pepin and the Pope's independence had been won over from the Emperor of Constantinople. Both the temporal and spiritual supremacy had been given of which Charlemagne would inherit and later become the Holy Roman Emperor of the Holy Roman Empire.

Pepin returned his gratitude to the Pope by driving out the Lombards from the lands of the Papal States and handed them over to the Church of St. Peter at Rome. He did not take the crown from the Lombards at this time but in terms of negotiations handed over the towns to the Holy See. The keys to the city were taken to Rome and laid at St. Peter's grave signifying the freedom from the Emperor of Constantinople and lord of the territories now known as the Papal States. The transformation of Roman rule in the Western Empire had slowly evolved to a Frankish kingdom that unified the populace through the Christian Church, Bishops, and Saints. From Gaul and the Merovingian Dynasty came a nation under the Carolingian Dynasty representing a moral stature with a high regard for cultural influences.

The life of Charles the Great was a golden era of religious celebrations, international intrigue, prosperity of the church, education, and culture. Charlemagne, as he was known, lived life to its fullest potential while completing every goal set forth to fulfill a Holy Roman Empire in the west. He would pass through all three phases of acceptance to be a Christian and then move to a fourth level that no other king proceeding the Roman Empire had done by becoming Holy Roman Emperor. Baptism would be the first ceremony given and the first of four acceptances by Charlemagne during his reign. Pope Hadrian baptized him with several family members in Rome in 781. The other three acceptances of intellectual, bringing forth Christianity to the kingdom, and becoming the Holy Roman Emperor was practiced throughout the rest of his reign as king of the Franks. The intellectual acceptance of Christianity was of great importance to Charlemagne who spent most of his time in regards to this matter. This included celebrating Easter and Christmas with his relatives in different areas of the kingdom.

Accounts are made by Nithard's Annals that he celebrated the holy days in Aachen, Quierzy, and Rome.

Charlemagne's character can only be told by what is known from the text given by his loyal scholar Einhard. His works portray Charlemagne as a man without need for monetary gains. In this regard he gave land to many and the laborers to work it. He won civil obedience throughout his vast Empire by the force of his own divine will, which all regarded to be the strength and unifying force of the kingdom. Charlemagne had great fortitude to bear and endure whatever came without yielding to deceitful minds or fortune given by those who did not have the same gains in mind for the kingdom. The difficulties he encountered did not deter him from a task but only strengthened his determination in advancing upon his enemies more effectively and with great wisdom.

Education of the royal household during the time of Charlemagne was bestowed upon a Celtic from York, England named Alcuin. He taught on a wide range of topics including wisdom, grammar, dialectics, rhetoric, mathematics, music, medicine, and astronomy. The liberal arts were to be learned at an early age in the royal household. Understanding of these was the main goal of the educator, not mastery level. The boys at a later age would learn horsemanship as well as military practices while the daughters of the king would learn the art of clothes making. History was a subject used for education in the royal court. One story goes while reading Virgil's story about the Trojans Charlemagne remembered an ancestor named Anchius. During the usual question and answer sessions he asked Alcuin if this could be a link to Aeneas father Anchises of the Trojans who traveled the seas to Italy. Language is what interested Charlemagne the most and he questioned Alcuin for as much knowledge as possible on this subject of Latin, which was the language of choice. Charlemagne gave a task to Alcuin to write a Bible for him that could be read by all his court and family. Alcuin did finish the Bible and upon so copies were to be made for all to read. This was not the only book Charles spent time reading, for "City of God" by St. Augustine was his favorite book to read. The Academy as it would come to be called was held outside in the countryside, churches, and the royal household at Worms.

Einhard took over the duties of Alcuin who retired to a monastery in Tours in 799 and became the part of the royal court soon after his studies in the monastery of Fulda in the Frankish homeland. He would later take up the task of writing down his ideas and memories of Charlemagne, which he considered a necessary obligation to a legend he so revered and yet feared he would not succeed in properly completing the task. The books he has written about Charlemagne and his times are the most insightful books of the Frankish age.

To bring the word to the people Charlemagne had books brought to the Royal household from abroad to be copied and distributed to the churches to be studied by the populace. He also adopted the idea of baptizing his enemies and building churches in the areas of the christianized people afterwards. His actions on this matter came soon after being crowned king of the Franks. Undertaking the duties of his father he had an assembly at Worms to insure the loyalty was upheld by the Bavarians, which was also of great importance to the Pope who also sent his emissaries to the assembly. Charlemagne had an oath to be sworn by all and it was expected to be upheld. If not soon after would come quick retribution with full military power and mercy if necessary.

The struggles Charlemagne faced during his time from 754 – 814 were many with few losses fought mainly against the Aquintane's, Lombards, Saxons, Danes, and Hun- Avar's. His first test in battle would come against Hunold in Aquitania where he would find quick victory and build a castle there called Fronsac. The next campaign would be against the Lombards in Italy where he defeated King Desiderius and sent him and his son out of Italy with no hopes of regaining any power there. Charlemagne then placed his son Pepin in charge of all of Italy and restored the rights of lands to the Romans. The Saxon War would be the next task undertaken which would last thirty-three years before they submitted to the King of the Franks. The war took so long due to the ferocity of the Saxons in battle and their ongoing settling of terms and then renunciation of terms afterwards. The determination of Charles never wavered on this front for he would continue to send out his counts into battle after each time the terms were breached. He would even enter into battle himself to make amends in these regards. The two examples of these were at Detmold (Mount Osning) and on the bank of the river Hase where the Saxons were routed and later scattered amongst the lands of the Franks. Final terms given to the warring Saxons were to accept the Christian faith, stop the worship of devils and idols, and come into union with the Frankish people.

One of the most bloody and spirited wars fought under the reign of Charlemagne was the Hun-Avar war in Pannonia. This war lasted seven years and yielded much treasure while at the same time being devastating to the land and totally wiping out the nobility of the region. All these wars had one purpose and result: to bring the people into the Holy Roman Empire and become a Christianized populace.

The Frankish army used during battles against rivals of the Frankish Kingdom and the Holy Roman Empire was small yet well organized and well paid for their victories. It numbered in the tens of thousand and was broken up into counts, vassal owners, heavy calvary, light calvary, and the men afoot.

The battle strategy was to scout out the enemy and produce necessary maps, and once the king and generals came to a battle strategy the elite military would move to the front and stage an initial attack. All battles would begin with a mass giving blessing upon the king, army, and the battleground itself. This presented the idea that God in His divine will was sending the army into battle to win victory for Christianity.

The Franks saw the European map of the time showing the mainland areas as Alamnia, Dacia, Germania, Saxonia, Fresia, Grecia, Gallia, Italia, Scotia, and Britania. Within this is the Frankish Empire, which was divided into four regions of Francia, Germania, Aquitaine, and Italy. Both the harshness of the terrain and the diversity of the language made travel difficult within the Frankish Kingdom and beyond its borders. In order to make travel and battle plans more effective, maps were drawn up by both military commanders and the Papal States. As the lands of the Frankish Kingdom expanded from 754 – 814 so did Christianity with the Papal States centered between it and the Byzantine Empire in Constantinople.

Charlemagne's first major determination in regards to the Papal States was against the Lombardy revolt, which Pope Hadrian had asked his help putting down. This was done is short manner by the Frank military upon which he took the Lombardy crown for himself and made the lands part of the Frankish Kingdom and sent the persons charged into exile. At the same time events in the Byzantine Empire to the east in Constantinople were slowly deteriorating and the Pope could not rely on the alliance with them. The Pope as well as the commonwealth needed a Christian Patricium for the Roman Papal States. The ability to unite the Teutonic races under one religion and one scepter was the ideal solution for the Papal States and divine decision later.

The fourth acceptance would be filled with grandeur as well as mystery – a divine mystery. On Christmas Day 801 A.D. in the basilica of St. Peter where Charlemagne was celebrating the birth of Christ. This was an event after the mass not foreseen by him or His Holiness Pope Leo who recognized the first Holy Roman Emperor by placing the diadem on Charlemagne's bowed head. Charles The Great, son of Pepin, king of the Franks, protector of the Papal States, was now Emperor of the Western Empire. Augustus, Holy Roman Emperor, crowned by God alone to be lord of peace, life, and victory. A divine moment handed down not by the Pope or taken by Charlemagne but given by God in an unforeseen moment in the most holy of places and where the last Roman Emperor stood three hundred years earlier. The shadow of the past now slowly disappeared along with the struggles endured to reach the grand event, at which God looked down in just agreement to His will. The crowning seemed a natural event with the Pope bestowing the crown as an instrument of God's will and the Roman people not only simply accepting the appointment, but praising and rejoicing over it. Thus all three -- the king, Pope, and people – were obeying the divine nature and providence of the event. They only looked to the harmony it would bring to all in the future.

Soon after this event in Aachen 802 the Emperor revised the laws which stated that every person from the age of twelve were to swear an oath of fidelity as an act of allegiance to the king. It was publicly explained that the oath meant each person was to live to his best effort to the services of Christianity. This meant no person could rightfully seize any goods or servants of the Emperors while he is so crowned and not to do harm in anyway to any administrator of the Christian Church, as the Emperor is its protector. The next area of government was the connection of church and state. Bishops, abbots, dukes, counts were all interconnected under the supreme rule of the Christian Emperor. Each had the right of jurisdiction but at the same time a binding obligation to the Emperor especially during battle against enemies of Christianity was expected.

Powers of the Holy Roman Emperor were unlimited in scope and were designated the headship and lordship of the world wherever he may reign. The coronation of Charlemagne bestowed upon him the transformation of an empire from godly Roman to Holy Roman with full succession of powers as Augustus. Charles the Great would use the powers vested in him to renew the aggressive stance against the uncivilized world with the war of the cross and the sword. This would be done through building of monasteries, fortresses, baptisms, and recognition of royal positions throughout the empire. A strong central government with the rule of law and unity throughout the empire with the aid of Christianity was the binding force that made the Holy Roman Empire a soaring eagle in the west. It was an extension of what Alexander the Great had achieved in the east fourteen centuries earlier. The spirit and determination that Charlemagne put into the transformation of the Western Empire by military, education, culture, churches, and court appointments was on such a great magnitude there was no match for it by any Ceasar in Roman times. His tireless energy in all aspects to make life better for all under the Christian religion would bring him to all corners and remote areas of the empire from Saxony, Spain, Slavia, Italy, and Pannonia.

Both decisions and articles based on them from wide-ranging and important matters were usually conducted under counsel of general assemblies. The assemblies brought to it the aid of counts, bishops, vassals, and even troops. Charlemagne never acted without taking counsel through his general assemblies, which could be one of the reasons he had so victories on the battlefield and amongst his royal court throughout the kingdom. Many administrative decisions and ceremonies were held during assemblies at different locations within the empire. The two most commonly used locations were Aachen, the capital that Charlemagne visited frequently, and Worms a central location in the empire. The administrative areas were military strategy, placing new counts and dukes in newly acquired territories, laws and judgments. Military decisions were frequently made at these assemblies by the Franks in order to come to a consensus on actions to be taken against threats to the empire. Ceremonies as well were conducted which included crowning of family members and receiving of foreign dignitaries. The assemblies were not a new event to the old Frankish customs but there were more wide-ranging topics to be handled now that an entire empire had to be dealt with.

The palace at Aachen (Aiz-la-Chapelle) held many assemblies under the reign of Charlemagne and was built with grandeur in mind as it was to be the Capital city. Master architect Odo built the palace in the Byzantine style. It was to resemble the Church of San Vitale in Ravenna, which was modeled after the Holy Sepulcher in Jerusalem. The palace itself contained many sections in which to either conduct the general assemblies or for leisure purposes and included the main chapel, atrium, lateral basilicas, judgment hall, military barracks, royal living quarters, baths, and a choir room. Aachen Palace has three distinct features which creates its grandeur. The fact that it was built on Roman bath ruins gives it a place of ancient history from the time they ruled the lands. The secondary purpose of the palace was a mausoleum, giving it a holy appearance. The third feature was the treasures it housed including the swaddling clothes of the infant Jesus, the cloak of Virgin Mary at the Nativity, and the loincloth that Jesus wore during the Crucifixion. Besides Aachen (Aix-la-Chapelle) the preferred palaces by Charlemagne were Meuse of Herstal, Duren, Frankfurt, and Worms. He also had palaces built in Ingelheim in Mainz, Nijmegen at Waal, and one at Paderborn in Saxony. The palaces were built to be a functional part of the Frankish government but still provided the comforts needed to the royal family and the assemblies. They were a symbol of both religious diet and power during the Charlemagne Empire and many Emperors afterwards.

The second most powerful symbol of government on religious activity in the Frankish Empire was the abbeys and the bishops who ran them. The bishops held great power within the kingdom and both raised income as well as dealt it out for payment of building its religious structures throughout the kingdom. The bishops appointed by the King were of great importance when selection time came to bestow the honor upon the next in a vacated position. These appointments were carefully scrutinized by the king for the urban communities lived solely by the bishop's orders and for his agenda.

A Holy War would be conducted after the coronation of Charlemagne against the enemies of the Franks and the Holy Roman Empire. The main focus was converting all to Christianity with the granting of mercy in return.

The two main rivalries in this would be the Saxons of the northeast and the Danes. Charlemagne used many tactics to subdue the constant intrusions into the lands of the Franks including the military, building of walls, tearing down of idols and replacing with churches, and finally baptism of their main leader Witukind.

Chieftain of the Saxon, Witukind, vowed never to give land or soul to the Franks across the Rhine River. Charles was however more determined than ever to conclude this never-ending battle with the Saxons. Witukind proved to be more than elusive but practically invisible due to the lack of contact with him or his army as the Frankish forces scoured the lands in pursuit. After pursuit did not work, Charlemagne tried to win over the Saxons by following their traditions while at the same time bringing them over to his side. An Edict was drawn up giving out laws for any injustice done against the Frankish people much in accord with the same laws the Saxons had for their own injustices. Upon this Edict Charlemagne gave safe passage to Witukind to meet with a ceremony of baptism for him with an exchange of hostages for his safe travel. Full ceremony was given to this baptism with Charlemagne attending, which then concluded the long struggle between the opposing parties. Witukind was taken into the Frankish lands and was never heard or seen of again. A man of many great qualities Charles the Emperor showed his supreme wisdom in resolving difficult times as he had with the Lombards but with tactics only necessary for each situation.

The Holy Roman Empire began with Charlemagne and the title of Holy Roman Emperor would continue for almost eleven more centuries, all with the same common cause. He was more than just a legend but also a central idea in the minds of many and a Saint to others. The Eastern Germans would later claim him as *Imperium Teutonici* in respect of all the regions he reigned over and different races as well. Others would go farther than this and claim him as *Imperium Romanorum, Imperium Christianum, Imperium Francorum* all in respects to the Roman Papacy he defended, Christianity he supported, and France he administered.

The crowning of Charlemagne and the creation of The Holy Roman Empire was an historical event that still has resonant effects today. He changed the direction of the people from barbarism, ungoverned people, disorder, separation, disunity, paganism, and dark ages. There are many stories about the life of this great champion of Christianity but no one story can explain the joy and excitement he created by his own will. And no one person could recreate a parallel one in its entirety. A true Christian is a person who gives alms to his fellow citizens, his church, and the individuals in need. Charlemagne upheld this as Holy Roman Emperor by sending many treasures and monetary gains to St. Peter's Church, the Pope, the poor in Egypt, Africa, and the Mediterranean region. His hopes would be to gain a wider area of Christian followers for the Holy Roman Empire and the Church. After his death the crown would come down by many means: inheritance, Pope's choice, and declaration of individuals within the Holy Roman Empire. However, none could gain the total support needed to unite as Charlemagne.

The Byzantine Empire although in turmoil was still a formidable military power and claimed the title of Roman Emperor although the Pope was at odds and did not need their services anymore. Charlemagne tried to win either transference of power, recognition, or possible marriage agreement. Neither of these was to come but the debate over supremacy and the Papal States would not always be at the center of each attention. Many gifts were given to the Franks by the East including an organ and elephant, Abul Abbas. Irene, the Byzantine Impress, exchanged many correspondences with the Holy Roman Emperor during her troubled reign. Whether there was a marriage proposal at anytime is not known. However, it would not be the intention of Charlemagne at this time to try to combine the two empires since he was already drawn into more important battles and probably another in the East would come from this arrangement. The Byzantine Empire succeeded with the title Roman Emperor the accompanying title of Patriarch to Jerusalem and the keys to the Holy Sepulcher and the banner of Calvary. This would bring forth in the future many crusades headed by the Holy Roman Emperor as well as kings from many areas of Europe.

The divine framework of the Holy Roman Empire and the purpose of each are for the authority over both the soul and the body with unity between them here on earth. The Pope ordained by God is given the authority over the souls of mortals and reigns above the administration of bishops and priests. The Emperor ordained by God is given the authority over the body of mortals and reigns above the administration of the counts and dukes. Thus, the body does not act without the soul and the soul cannot act without the body one any stronger than the other except in the will of the soul itself. Therefore, the Pope cannot act without the aid of the Emperor and the Emperor cannot act without the aid of the Pope. One was no stronger in power than the other, but the will of God acting through the Pope. The Pope handles spiritual and eternal matters and the Emperor strives to gain the same common end through dealings with one another and temporal and mortal matters. The two missions of the Emperor are to keep the peace while being a patriarch to the church abroad. Thus, the Emperor is given a more sacred character than earlier Roman Emperors with religious ties and removing the bindings of birth and place of origin that also came with the old Roman Empire. Therefore, the Holy Roman Empire and the Holy Roman Church join in Christianity and

Romanism where Rome is the origin and capital where the Holy See resides. There can be no opposition between the two because both serve the same higher purpose, which is absolute and never changing. Bound by the same will, neither can be over the other since one serves the spiritual, the other the temporal and cooperation of each is needed for the welfare of all.

Pepin, the son of Charlemagne, was the king of Italy whose duties were to defend against any attacks upon the state and the Pope. Fleets from Greece, Spain and Africa were a constant threat to Venice, Dalmatia, Corsica and Sardina, and the Italian coastline. Bernard, grandson of Charlemagne, was also sent to Italy to support his position there and was made King of Italy after his father had died. This occurred in 813 while at the same time in Aachen Louis, king of Aquitaine, son of the Emperor was crowned and shared the title with his father. Upon his death he reconciled the treasures of the palace with his brothers, his sisters, and Bernard. His brothers were to remain in the palace, his sisters sent to a monastery, and Bernard was to be king of Italy. The disputes over the crown would begin here, for reasons mostly of lack of action by two parties. One, the lack of the qualities of Louis of which Clovis and Charlemagne showed by quickly putting down any possible attempts to lay claim to the crown. Secondly, there was no divine ceremony in Rome of the crowning of Louis bestowing full honors unto the Emperor as had been with Charlemagne. There was however another type of divine intervention, which needs to be mentioned, and that is compromise and reconciliation.

Louis put all the above mentioned into monasteries and at the same time made his son Pepin king of Aquitaine, Louis Bavaria, and Lothar Emperor with him and after his death. Another son Charles was born later and was granted his share of the kingdom that he wanted. This would be a decision that would become a disruption within the family for some time. Louis sided with Charles on this decision, causing Pepin and Lothar to take action. They took both of them into free custody, bringing things to a higher stage of conflict. Louis relented to their wishes by promising better rule by reconstructing the government in relation to religious worship while pardoning each for their actions. He so agreed and land was again redistributed amongst members of the royal family.

Another struggle would begin with skirmishes amongst each side who maneuvered from one position within the kingdom to the next to get an upper hand. Envoys with letters of agreement were sent from one party to the next. On June 20 Louis Holy Roman Emperor died in Mainz and buried in Metz at St. Arnulf's. All parties had distanced themselves, Lothar in Italy, Louis in the Rhine area, and Charles in Aquitaine. Charles and Louis were now looking for a divine judgment to the situation and both swore an oath of rightful treatment upon their brother and each other in return. Emissaries were sent out to Lothar and he accepted the oaths of peace and the division of the kingdom into three parts of which he had his choice as Emperor. They proceeded to thank the Almighty God that justice had prevailed for all parties.

By no means did the breakup of the empire affect the administration. Instead, it increased the resolve in all regions needed to strengthen it further. England, Spain, Jerusalem and the East would now become of greater importance to all parties as well as the Holy Roman Emperor. The Byzantine Empire and the Holy Roman Empire united in struggles outside their realms in the form of the Crusades. The spread of Christianity and its defense would be shared by the three lines of descendants of Charlemagne. The Plantagenets', Arundell's, and Howard's all were born from the line of the Franks and all would strive to continue what Charlemagne had started in Rome, Italy on Christmas Day 801.

Zeus
Sanne Smit

Clovis the Great
Francois-Louis Dejuinne (1786 – 1844)

Charlemagne, Charles the Great
Holy Roman Emperor

Adeliza of Louvania
Henry Colburn

Edward I Plantagenet
Westminster Abbey (1272 – 1307)

John Howard
Duke of Norfolk

Katherine Howard
Queen of England

Rudolph II
Holy Roman Emperor
Johann (1600- 1603) or Hans von Aachen (1552-1616)
Kunsthistorisches Museum, Vienna, Austria
Bridgeman Art Library

Anne Arundell
Louis P. Dieterich after Van Dyke
Maryland Historical Society Library

Franics II
Holy Roman Emperor
Austria 1792

Phillip Howard

V

PLANTAGENET

Urban began by stressing reform, by renewing the Truce of God,
and by pleading for peace among the nobility. Then came the
real purpose of the assembly. The Crusades on behalf of pious
Christians in Jerusalem.

Pope Urban II, "Christendom and Christianity in the
Middle Ages", Adrian H. Bredero 105, 106

THE AGE OF CHARLEMAGNE would be continued by his descendants who
were supremely devoted to chivalry, ruling over their lands, Christianity and
crusades to the Holy Land. These descendants of Charlemagne would pride
themselves on being the optimum and most efficient soldiers of their time,
acquiring vast wealth and lands as well as international recognition. Their
main objective from the three acceptances of Christianity was bringing it
forth to the people and nothing would stand in their way in doing so. The
House of Anjou, which would later bring forth the Plantagenets, was founded
on the semi-legendary soldier of fortune Ingelgar. He had great military
prowess and won victories that helped him obtain estates in the Loire Valley
of France. In 941 the Count of Anjou was established, creating a long line
of rulers in the Western part of France that would be increased not only in
France over time but also in England. This line of extraordinary men would
help create prosperity, legendary stories, grand castles, memorable battles, and
Kings of Jerusalem.

When the empire that Charlemagne had created was split up, West Francia
was ruled by Charles the Bald son of Louis The Pious and brother in law to
Lothar 1. During the next century the Carolingian Dynasty collapsed and with
it came Hugh Capet and the Capetians. The Capetians were recognized kings
of France and anointed by the archbishop of Reims. Hugh Capet was elected
to his position as King of France by the counts within the kingdom. These

counts would ironically become his main rivals in power, and to overcome the election debate in the future he made his son Robert his heir as King of France . There were great vassals within the kingdom of France and one was held by Count of Anjou. These vassals were ruled in a pyramid shape hierarchy with the Count ruling over all the lands he owned. The King of France held only limited power over these counties and duchies from his reigning area of Paris and the powerful Counts of Anjou, Blois, and Normandy would show their power in their respective regions through alliances, battles, and political jousting. The Count of Anjou would overshadow each and assembled lands that were far greater than the Royal House.

Fulk Nerra (Fulk III) was the great-great-grandson of Ingelgar and a man of great extremes in both policy and purpose while being a devout Christian in remarkable ways. He won battles with great devastation to the enemy to enable him to gain their full support such as the one to the west in Brittany. He was a Christian of highest esteem and showed this by traveling to Jerusalem three times, Rome at least once, and founded two abbeys, Beaulieu-les-Loches near Tours, and St. Nicholas at Angers. Fulk Nerra died while returning from his last visit to Jerusalem but not before stamping the trademark of the Counts of Anjou and the Plantagenets for generations to come.

The black monks of the abbeys St. Benedictine, St. Alban, Durham, Glastonbury, and Peterborough were put in control of the spiritual and material welfare of their community. Each monk was expected to live a rigorous routine of prayer, reading and labor. These abbeys were also very wealthy at the time of the Counts of Anjou, Plantagenets and Normans, and had great influence amongst the rulers and administrators within the area they served.

Fulk V, great-grandson of Fulk Nerra, was a devout Christian and vigorous in his dealings with other counts including Henry I. He obtained Maine by marrying the count's daughter and from there he continued to acquire land by putting down the unjust which included Touraine. In 1128 Baldwin II, King of Jerusalem, came to France to gain help from King Louis VI and to find a favorable husband for his daughter Melisande and eventually become the King of Jerusalem. Baldwin II was the defender of the Holy Sepulcher and was looking for the right candidate to hand it over when he had passed on. The King of France had only one candidate he thought was up to the task and that was Fulk V. He had already made a trip to Jerusalem and possessed all the necessary traits of a great leader including being faithful, a powerful ruler, patient and experienced military soldier, and wisdom in uniting. Fulk V after his marriage to Melisande now co-ruled as monarch over the Latin kingdom of Jerusalem.

Anjou is known as the garden of France and it lies in the fertile Loire valley on the east side of France where there are cool ocean breezes and a gentle climate in which to live. Angers is the capital city of Anjou and was inhabited by the ruling Angevins. The river Maine flows through the town and many types of fruits and flowers can be found there. To keep these fertile lands the Count of Anjou had to show his honor and ability to keep them militarily as well as politically. Knighthood would become the necessary means for achieving this objective. While his father had been chosen to be King of Jerusalem, Geoffrey V was winning his honor in tournaments. During one tournament held between the Normans and the Bretons he led his men to the front lines in battle of clashing of arms, yelling of men to arms, and pounding of horses and inflicted many casualties upon the adversary. This display of knighthood gave him quite a measure of fame and he continued to seek out tournaments in Flanders to hone his skills in battle.

Castles were a major strong point as well for military purposes, which started with Fulk Nerra. He used the strategy of positioning castles where it could be used as a base for launching attacks as well as fortification against his enemies. These castles formed lines of communication as well as important centres. Among these were the Treves on the river Loire and the Durtal on the Loire above Angers. Some thirteen castles were built during this time period of Fulk of Anjou, the earliest stone fortifications built in the Middle Ages.

In the eleventh century, around Fulk Nerra's time, the Pope had become an insignificant figure but by the age of Fulk V he had restored his leadership of Christendom beginning a new age and new direction for all Christians. The Byzantine Empire was being besieged along with the Holy Land troubling all parties including the Eastern and Western Empires and the Pope himself. Pope Urban II was looking to reunite the Eastern Empire into Papal Supremacy and at the same time strengthen the Christian forces. Urban II for this reason called for two councils in 1095 in Milan, Italy and Clermont, France. The Pope asked for peace amongst the nobility and a Truce of God. In his message to the council he addressed the distress amongst the pilgrims in Jerusalem and asked for the aid of the knights and the pious Christians. A great cry went out to do the will of God and fight for the honor of the cross which would then be called "Crusade". This appeal went out to the nobility and the people with the leadership of the Pope. On July 15, 1099 the First Crusade retook Jerusalem after many hardships. The taking up of the cross by peasants, noblemen, counts, kings, and Holy Roman Emperors would begin from this victorious crusade.

The first Crusade stirred memories of the long-forgotten knights of Charlemagne, which gave way to an era of French nationalism. Roland was one of these knights who took up arms for the King of the Franks in a march into Spain in 778 to put down what was thought to be a necessary battle to hold off enemy incursions into the Frankish kingdom. The battle did not fare well on that occasion for the Franks maybe due to the lack of foresight into enemy strength, terrain, and alliances. During the march back to the homeland with a long train of horses and wagons behind them, an attack was made upon the lines in the rear. Charlemagne, who was leading his army out of Spain, was being trailed in the rear by his great knight Roland. The attack was unexpected and concluded with the loss of many good soldiers including Roland who took it upon himself to make sure all others made it out safely even with the loss of his own life. The "Song of Roland" about the knights of Charlemagne was sung and the people of France would begin to sing it again for the Crusades.

In 1128 Geoffrey V Plantagenet married Matilda a Dowager, Empress and daughter of Henry I of England. Henry I promised the succession of England to his daughter but Stephen of Blois seized the kingdom bringing the Plantagenets and him into a struggle many times over. Geoffrey V Plantagenet was knighted in great ceremony with all the gifts, horses, clothing and amour befitting one for his first campaign of many. Geoffrey's first conquest would be Normandy in 1144, which would bring his land of Maine and Anjou into the consolidation of Eastern France. The claim to England thus was binding in that many nobles held land on both sides of the Channel and Geoffrey was now Duke of Normandy.

Upon the death of Geoffrey Plantagenet in 1151 his son Henry II became Duke of Normandy and Count of Anjou. He soon after married Eleanor, the former wife of Louis VII King of France. The marriage meant the inheritance of Aquitaine, adding to the immense area of France in the possession of the Plantagenets, enough to be more powerful than the King of France. This marriage would create the greatest period of the Plantagenet generations, as Eleanor was as formidable as Henry II when it came to politics and battles. Their marriage was celebrated at the cathedral in Poitiers, which was rebuilt in Gothic style having the usual characteristics of being spacious, domed, ribbed, luminous, and in one window artwork showing of the crucifixion of both Christ and St. Peter.

In 1153 Henry II landed in England to face off with Stephen or to grant terms for the King of England. An agreement was reached that made Henry II the successor to Stephen, who died one year later. Pressure from the barons who sided with Henry II was enough to hand him what was given to Matilda. Henry II Plantagenet was now King of England, Duke of Normandy, Count of Anjou, and Duke of Aquintaine. This would not be the end of acquisitions, for more was gained at a future time including Northumbria, alliances with the Welsh, Ireland, and Vexin (France). This Angevin was a successful ruler with immense dominions who could easily rival the crown of the King of France.

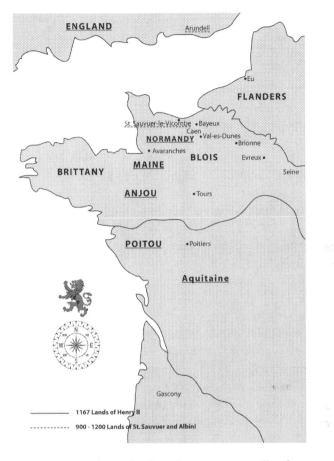

Henry II Plantagenet brought from his ancestor Fulk of Anjou the use of castles in his dominions. He built Dover Castle in Kent in 1167, Chateau of Gisors in Normandy, and expanded Chateau of Chinon in central France where Joan of Arc would eventually meet the Dauphin, the future Charles VII of France. These castles served to display his large wealth and his military presence in areas he wished to maintain.

Henry II was known for numerous respectful traits which many of his time came to admire. His characteristics lend him not only a great man but also a just Christian. . Policies used to reconstruct England were also very popular as Henry II took away all grants and titles handed down by Stephen and reshaped the appointments of the church, land, and castles, which would help restore the revenue and prosperity to the people along with peace.

There would become the same struggles between Henry II's sons after his death in 1170 as was when Charlemagne passed on his reign and lands to his sons. Henry was to inherit England, Normandy, and Anjou; Richard the Lionheart was to have Poitou; Geoffrey was to get Brittany; and John Lackland the youngest was left with no lands. A struggle of the same nature would begin as did under Louis the Pious but it would end in the same divine Christian way leaving the lesser as the King of England, John Lackland.

Both Henry and Geoffrey died at a young age and Henry II had to divide the wealth, land, and crown differently between Richard and John. He decided to give to Richard the land he had along with the land of the other brothers while John was to succeed him upon Henry II's death. This arrangement would not become an issue to Richard in the future for he had other plans that were of greater importance and would resolve the issue with his brother John at some other time.

When Richard was of the young age of twelve he was recognized as the Duke of Aquitaine in the church of St. Hillary of Poitiers. He would now become the heir to his mother's rich holdings in the South of France in the lush county of Poitou as he was his mother's favorite. The fertile lands of Poitier would be the home that Richard cherished more than anywhere else he traveled.

To defend his lands, Richard, as his father had before, built castles to guard against neighboring rivals and the King of France. In 1196-1198 he built Chateau Gaillard in Normandy on the river Siene near Les Andelys. The fortifications used to build the castle were learned during the Crusades. It was virtually impenetrable except for one side by besiegers. The policy of the Plantagenet was to destroy castles of unruly nobles while building other castles which suited their needs and rebuilding older ones. Castles would also become a major strategic fortification for Richard while on the Crusades. When he captured the island of Cyprus on the Fourth Crusade Mistra was built as a stronghold in the Mediterranean. In 1191 Richard took the castle in Casarea, which was founded by the Phoenicians and rebuilt by Herod and also occupied by different leaders several times. The ability to build castles was not the only strong point of the Plantagenet but overthrowing them was a military skill that would prove useful.

Richard the Lionheart (Coeur-De-Lion) was an enthusiast of the art of military weaponry and its use. He spent great deals of time honing his skills with the sword, lance, ax, and horse eventually becoming a master of the use of each. A knight with great military skills and strategy he would be able to win over others in leading them against large armies far greater than his. Defending Christendom and honoring ones' duties to his family and social order were learned early, being freely accepted far more than his brother John.

In 1177 Henry II and Richard the Lionheart met King Louis of France in Normandy to discuss terms of the Crusade and also the marriage of Alice his daughter. They put aside their differences and agreed that a Crusade was in order but marriage would be put aside until afterwards. During the time of planning the Crusade, Henry II was also dealing with the conflicts in Aquitaine he had spent much time on when not across the Channel in England. When he managed to take time for affairs in England, Richard would take up arms against the rivals and mutineers within their region. Henry II died before the Crusade was underway, leaving Richard to deal with the issue of defenses at home and the plans to crusade in Jerusalem. In Tours in 1187, after word of defeats and deaths in the Holy Land he decided to take the cross and made a vow as a crusader to free the Holy Lands. Richard enter into a pact which would require him to leave behind France and England and instead spend more time to generate the money and provisions necessary to travel on the perilous path to Jerusalem.

Another turn of events came when John was in England and had found a wife, Isabel, who he married. Richard on this occasion gave to John three counties in England, five castles, forests, villages and much more to show his faith in him and social status due to a brother of a king. This having been done Richard would now spend all the time he had in preparation of the Crusade.

There were approximately seven Crusades made to the Holy Land to free it from the hands of those who oppressed the pilgrims there. The first Crusade in 1099, although it incurred many losses, was successful. Crusader states were established in Jerusalem, Tripoli, and Antioch. The Franks and the Emperor of Constantinople were the two benefactors of this crusade. The two routes to be taken were by land or by sea, the latter would require large numbers of ships which were not available, thus early Crusades took a path by land. The route would take them through Contantanipole and onto Asia Minor and finally to the Holy Land. The second crusade suffered many losses during this route as the opposing armies saw them as more of a threat than before. The third Crusade would be led by Richard the Lionheart whose strategy and military prowess would win him and the Crusaders victory during the trip to Jerusalem and during the battles fought in the Holy Land. Richard spent a great deal of time away from is homeland in preparing for the third Crusade. Accompanying Richard on this crusade would be Philip II and Frederick I Barbarossa, the German Emperor, both of whom either did not make the full trip or left before the campaign was finished as did Philip II.

The first step of the third Crusade was to Messina in Sicily but before going there Richard made a stop at the mouth of the Tiber River near Rome where he met some clerics of the Pope and hoped his fleet of ships could rendezvous with him in time. Other stops where made in Naples and Salerno where Richard asked for medical advice for ills he frequently encountered.

He was now ready to catch up with his fleet in Messina. The arrival was a grand showing that was designed to impress the local nobility and their followers. His showing of control over the military as well as upstaging the accompanying Philip II was a calculated effort for future issues that might arise.

The next step was to cross the Mediterranean, which could not be done during the wintertime, thus they chose to stay and rest for the upcoming task. Before moving on, the military was trimmed down by eliminating the men who were less useful and less battle ready, making a lighter and faster travel to the next destination, Crete. In 1191 they set sail with Richard's fiancee Berengaria and his sister Joan. Upon arrival at Crete there were to his dismay missing ships so he thus sailed onto Rhodes to search for them. A second leg was to Cyprus where King Richard met issues with the reigning king but upon resolving them between each other it was made clear that Richard was the commander of his as well as the Latin army taken on the Crusade. A ceremony was also given before departure with the marriage of Berengaria to Richard, making her the Queen of England with the anointing of the bishop. This event took several days as Richard must have wanted to celebrate the event and rest and plan for the final leg of the journey to the Holy Land.

Cyprus brought the Crusade food, money, glory, and a staging place for land movements as well as support in case of crisis. Richard the Lionheart, King of England, heir of the Plantagenets would now set sail for the Holy Land and fulfill what he was trained to do since childhood. The ships arrived at Tyre and spent the night in the harbor before moving onto the Bay of Haifa and the city of Acre. His arrival was welcomed by all as he stepped ashore for the first time in the Holy land where his ancestor Fulk V had traveled before him. The alliances changed immediately in Richard's favor as he gained troops by showing daring in battle and generosity in the form of payment in gold coins. Only several days transpired with the battle of Acre before the defending army surrendered to Richard giving him terms in the form of negotiations. They included the return of prisoners, the Holy Cross, and the city released to the Latins.

Richard then headed south down the coast flanked by his ships on the coast. He went into the city of Jaffa with his knights, archers, and other armed forces and with scarce resistance brought down the defending army by the sword, ending the lives of many foes. Richard the Lionheart was known for his marvelous sword, which had a lion on each side of the gild and a cross on the top part of the handle knob. An attempt to capture Richard was made by several thousand enemy troops but before they could get close enough he was alerted and brought several companions with him to attack their center.

They were sent into confusion by this tactic and fled as Richard's men, eager for battle, dispersed them as a full day passed.

The Christians were now allowed free access to the city of Jerusalem in 1192 by the terms given upon the victory of Richard and his Crusaders, which at the time was the best that could be awarded in light of the fact that Acre and Jaffa were also in the hands of the Christians. Sixteen months had passed while in the Holy Land when Richard decided it was time to leave for the homeland as Henry of Champagne was given full control over the Latin Kingdom. In 1199 he died of a single arrow during battle in his homeland leaving his lands and King of England to John Lackland. Richard the Lionheart was a man of great stature who was devoted to Christianity and thus took it upon himself to make a difference in his homeland as well as on the Crusade. This devotion would be carried on by Edward I Plantagenet, the grandson of John Lackland.

Edward I, King of England, took up the cross in 1270 and sailed to Jerusalem with his wife Eleanor of Castile. Upon arrival of some one thousand men under his command into the besieged city the battle was joined and with fierce fighting they were able to retake the city. They then took Nazareth and Haifa, both moral and strategic victories. But with only of fraction of the men needed to obtain substantial gains, this Crusade would be known more for it magnificence than the significant difference it made over time in the Holy Land. A most courageous effort would end in a truce that was forged once again out of necessity for one side and respect given by the other. Edward I soon afterwards sailed back to England to begin the reformation necessary to create a prosperous and unified kingdom under his rule.

While traveling back to England from the victorious crusade Edward heard of the deaths of three family members. His son John had died from an illness, Henry III his father, and Richard de Cornwall his uncle. Richard de Cornwall was Count of Poitou, Earl of Cornwall, and King of the Romans. He was one of the wealthiest men in Europe at the time and upon his wife Isabel death he took up the crusade to the Holy Land. He played a role of reconstruction and prisoner negotiations but did not engage in battle as did Richard the Lionheart. He was made King of Germany and King of the Romans crowned by Pope Alexander IV in 1257. His sister Isabella was the Empress of Frederick II and daughter Joan de Plantagenet de Cornwall would marry Sir John Howard of the Norfolk Line. He was buried in Hayles Abbey of which he founded.

Edward I was crowned King of England with great ceremony which included being seated on the "Coronation Stone", Jacobs' "Pillar Stone", brought to England ages ago. This coronation was befitting of his reign which would show justice handed down by a proper king. He was convinced the law of the kingdom needed reformation and he made an appointment to the chancellor to assure this would be done.

Windsor Castle was the home of Edward I and Eleanor who would make use of its chambers, chapels and great halls built by Henry I in Norman style. The castle was built after the battle of Hastings in Berkshire, England 1165. Eleanor gave birth to an estimated fifteen children some of who may have died at an early age. Amongst them Alice, Eleanor, Margaret, Mary, Elizabeth, Blanche, Beatrice, Katherine, and Berengeria. There were later castles built in Wales including Conwy Aberystwyth, Beaumaris, Builth, Caernarvon, Flint, Harlech which were better built in the concentric system and interior finishing. These castles were constructed at the peak of modern castle building and at a time that Edward I was attempting to bring Wales into the kingdom of England.

Edward I maintained a system of government which included a triple representation of nobility, clergy, and the commons. The use of representation by commons was first used to gain support and confer on military issues during war time. This Parliament at Westminster met for the first time in 1295 and included men who represented the commons, seven earls, forty one barons, and two knights from each shire. The Parliament would deliberate separately by the three bodies which later became the House of Lords and the House of Commons. The decision of regular meetings at Westminster was brought about by necessity due to the hardships the Parliament had to endure to travel where the king was within the kingdom with little food and less than adequate place to meet usually a church. This arrangement united the Parliament and created more cohesion amongst the representatives in a central place without all the hardships associated with meeting in a chosen place given by the king wherever he may have been at the time.

Edward I will always be known for three main struggles he took on with great leadership codifying the laws, Scotland, and Wales. A superior Plantagenet he took on these issues as both a wise lawgiver and administrator but also as a great military leader who was determined to unite all ends of the kingdom. One story went he was told by the Welsh leaders he had no just cause to think there was any claim to the lands of Wales since he had never lived there or owned lands there. Edward I answered this by living in Wales with his wife long enough to have a son born there and afterwards proclaimed him the Prince of Wales.

A final issue that Edward I had to contend with was a battle between French and English as far as shipment of goods and rights to naval ports and naval lines of navigation. The Plantagenet still had thoughts of reuniting the old dominions of Anjou, Normandy, and Aquitaine and had Flander's as a chief ally. This ally was created long before Edward I time and is deep rooted within the Plantagenet, Howard, and Arundell lines. Resolvement between the two nations would not come by one naval battle, one military victory or a generation. The Hundred Years War as it became known lasted into the reign of Edward III and had effects that may have caused the start of the next war in England called the War of the Roses.

Events which would follow after Edward I would effect England in a dramatic way and his descendants starting with Edward III. Two other family lineage's would also be brought into conflict within the Plantagenet reign in part by the Crown, battles for the Crown, and marriages between the lineage's. The lineal descent from Edward I shows the marriages between the Plantagenet's, Howard's, and Arundell's bringing them royal honors and responsibilities to protect the Crown. On the side of Arundell the lineage from Edward I descends by Edward II marrying Isabella, Edward III marrying Phillipa of Hainault, John Gaunt marrying Katherine Swynford, Joan de Beaufort marrying Ralph Nevill, Richard Nevill marring Alice Moutacute, Katherine Nevill marrying Lord William Bonvile, Cecelia Bonvile marrying Thomas Grey Marquess Dorset, and Elizabeth Grey marring John Arundell X. The latter was the line of York from which Henry VII married Elizabeth of York. On the side of Howard the lineage from Edward I descends by Thomas Plantagenet marrying Alice Halys, Margaret Plantagenet marrying Lord John Mowbray, Thomas Mowbray marrying Elizabeth Fitz Alan, Margaret Mowbray marrying Robert Howard, John Howard (first Duke of Norfolk) marrying Katherine Moleyns, Thomas Howard (second Duke of Norfolk) marrying Elizabeth Tilney, and Edmund Howard marrying Joyce Culpepper. The last marriage would bring together the Arundell and Howard lineage's by Thomas Arundell, son of John Arundell X, marrying Margaret Howard. These lineage's from Edward I represent from England Henry III married Eleanor, from Spain Ferdinand III who married Joanna whose daughter was Eleanor of Castile, and from France Phillip III who married Mary of Brabant whose daughter was Margaret of France. These marriages would bring all three families both prominence and bitterness starting with the reign of Edward III. After the Hundred Years War there became conflict within the kingdom and the royal family. The events which caused these are numerable but they can be said to have led up to the War of the Roses and finally the Battle of Bosworth Field.

A time of turmoil came during the reign of Richard II who came to the throne in 1377 during a time of turbulence due to issues of taxation and revenue that were caused by the Hundred Years War with the French. His marriage to Anne, sister of Wenceslas of Bohemia King of the Romans, was thought to be very costly and secondly it was foreseen the knights and nobles were the only parties gaining from the war with France. A clash between the royal descendants of Edward III which included John Gaunt, Henry IV Lancastrian, and Richard II was set to see who would reign over a bad situation that was created during this time for England. In 1399 Henry IV overthrew the throne by the will of the people, the Church, and Parliament. This would begin the war between the Yorkist of John Gaunt who was seeking the throne for himself and the Lancastrians for the next hundred years.

In this struggle between the two descendant lines from Edward III, Lancastrians and the Yorks, the Crown would be taken over three times in two major battles St. Alban's the opening of the War of the Roses and the Battle of Bosworth Field ending the war. Both Henry IV and Henry V would reign until overthrown by the troops of Richard III and then he would eventually become overthrown in battle at Bosworth by Henry VII. The Duke of Norfolk, Howard, was sided with the Yorkist and of Edward III and Richard III throughout the battles against the Lancastrians. The Arundell's were known for their great battle readiness and knighthood sided with the Lancastrians due to the case against Edward III for being incapable of ruling and Richard III committing an unlawful act against his own family. After the battle of St. Albans Arundell would pay for his attacks against the Crown as would Howard after the battle at Bosworth Field.

The reign of the Plantagenets would come to and end at Bosworth Field in 1485 but not without any less valor in battle as the first Plantagenet Geoffrey V. Chilvary in battle was what brought the Plantagenets the Crown and it is how their reign would end but the heart of the Plantagenet dynasty was their great will to spread the Christian faith to as many regions as they could while governing a kingdom at odds with this position. A dynasty of the magnitude of the Plantagenets could certainly be said as the last great dynasty on both the French and English regions and can possibly only be matched in the next century on the European Continent by the Austrian Habsburgs.

VI

HOWARD

It is nobler to receive a sword and belt from a man of God for the fittest man to consecrate the soldier of an earthly king is the soldier of Christ.

Hereward, "Hereward the Wake" Charles Kingsley 89

THE HOWARDS' ANCESTRY FOLLOWS that of the Plantagenet lineage from a great king of the Franks, followed by an honorable knight, and then by just and noble men having strong beliefs in the Catholic faith. Their lineage played a substantial role in England's history as they held the Dukedom of Norfolk and Earldom of Arundell. They had many honours bestowed on them and this lineage held many peerages, but adversity would be endured for their protection to the Crown. The Howard surname starting with Hereward of Bourne has roots that can be found as far back as 1054 in England and to this the day the family continues to hold their noble position within England's Nobility and the Holy Roman Empire.

The Howard family has its roots in both Frankish and Anglo-Saxon ancestry, and to better understand their role it must first be presented in the context of the history of England as it has transferred from one ruling race to the next over 1300 years. The Romans were the first to occupy the lands of the Celtic and Welsh people in the year 100 AD and would continue their stronghold until 500 AD. The legendary story of King Arthur is somehow interwoven in the later stage of the Roman occupancy with his "Knights of the Round Table". They were trained by the Romans to defend the land against attacks by regional forces and invading armies from across the coast. The pullout by the Romans due to the deteriorating position in Rome left King Arthur and his knights alone to defend against the next invading force across the Channel which was the Anglo-Saxons. The fate of Arthur and his knights is not clear and is beyond this text, but the Anglo-Saxons took advantage of a lack of unity to defeat them in battles as they progressed from the north to the south and possession of Britain was nearly complete by the seventh century.

Another invading army would be the Danes or Northmen from the European peninsula. They fought with great determination and ultimately conquered the English Anglo-Saxons and took northern England. Their attempt to destroy the churches and monasteries almost extinguished learning in the areas they occupied. In 1066 the Anglo-Saxons would be once again defending against invaders, this time the Normans under William the Conqueror, Duke of Normandy. His victory at Hastings gained him control and kingship over the lands putting the Norman French in political favor. The Crown would later be handed over to the French Plantagenets and Geoffrey V would be the first in many generations to reign.

England during 770 AD was comprised of many different regions: Northumbria, Angles, Mercia, Wessex, and Welsh. The Danes held control of the Northumbria and Angles regions while the Anglo-Saxons controlled most of Mercia and Wessex to the south. The first king of Wessex under Anglo-Saxon rule was Egbert, who married a Frankish Princess and sister-in-law to Charlemagne. His reign from 802-839 was very successful in consolidating territory under Anglo-Saxon rule after he had spent some time period in the Frankish court since being expelled by opposition leaders Offa and Beorhtric. Upon Egbert's return he crushed Welsh rebellion, in particular Cornwall, then defeated Beornwulf in Mercia. Victories came quickly for the new king afterwards in Kent, Surrey, Sussex, and Essex. Egbert considered Cornwall his stronghold in the region to fight against any naval invasion, the Welsh to the west, and the Danes to the north until an army could be dispatched to drive them out. Egbert was buried in Winchester, Hampshire and was generally called *Bretwalda* (British Ruler). His grandson Egbert III would carry on his mission to keep the Danes out of the British Isles and consolidate power under Christian rule. This was possibly done by the use of Frankish military tactics and he was presumably in contact with the Frankish Royal Court since he was married to Redburh, a possible daughter of Charlemagne and Frastrada.

In 871 King Alfred the Great would enter into a battle for his kingdom that would change England into a system that mirrored the one taking place across the Channel in Western Europe. The Danes would invade in 865 with little or no resistance, forcing the regions of Mercia and Northumbria in the north to sue for peace, the usual agreement for the period. Alfred would be pulled into the war when they moved into Wessex in the south and in turn he would also have to sue for peace. The cause of this was due to the inability of the regions and people to unite as one against the invading army. Alfred's vision and intelligence would alter the course of events only after he was sent into full retreat within the forest of Wessex.

Alfred the Great had a thirst for knowledge that started at an early age, hence his father sent him to Rome which was expected to help him gain some spiritual experience. He traveled to Rome, and was twice received by Pope Leo IV who accorded him with honours. On the second trip to Rome he traveled through the Frankish kingdom where they were met by Charles the Bald. During this stay Alfred's father Aethelwulf married Charles' daughter Judith while he spent time wandering amongst the abundance of scholars within the Frankish kingdom. The probable impact this had on Alfred in later years was the wealth of knowledge he thought could be passed on to his own kingdom. He also saw how the Frankish kingdom was able to deal with the Danish raids they had withstood. In 886 the same invading army attacked the western part of France, entering into the Seine river heading up to Paris where they were met with Frankish fortifications they could not overcome and left. These ideas along with the mutual faith of Christianity held by Alfred would help him transform his kingdom into a more unified and learned one.

In 878 the army of the Danes invaded Wessex into Devon with the intent of capturing Alfred, who was staying at his royal estate in Chippenham. The arrival of the attacking army was totally unexpected as there was a standing truce being honored by both leaving Alfred with no choice but to flee into the forest until he could gather his own forces to bear. He made fortifications in Athelney to plan his return and course of action against the invaders. Athelney would become the royal fortress for Alfred throughout his lifetime.

Alfred's plan of unification of Mercia and Wessex would begin by his marriage to a noble woman who was the daughter of Aethelred. The marriage was to seal and bind each region in a dual attack against the invading army. Alfred and his brother, who went to Mercia near Nottingham, gathered an immense army and while unable to breach the enemy's position was able to win peace between the two rivals. The Englishmen would now submit an oath of allegiance to follow Alfred their leader in any endeavor to defeat the invading army. In about 880 Alfred's unification of Mercia, Wessex and other parts of the kingdom would gain him recognition as King of the Anglo-Saxons. His strategic plan was to bring Christianity to all, divide his army into units, create a burgh system of fortification, send out scouts to find enemy positions to prevent their escape, and to build long ships to defeat the enemy's constant naval invasions.

Long ships built to defeat the invading naval forces were twice as long, faster, and higher above the water than the rival ships. The purpose of these ships seems to be a tactic of running the invading ships onto the beach and then attacking them with an army waiting along the shore. This tactic was very effective inland and had significant effect in winning such decisive victories that the Danes due to hardships inflicted upon them versus their gains began to retreat. In 878 during the victory over the Danes, Alfred used a tactic long ago used by Charlemagne against the Saxons by baptizing their leader Guthrum and making a treaty of law that would be recognized on both sides. This tactic would not have lasting effect on the Danes but it would bring many over to the side of the Englishmen.

Alfred was a devoted Christian and kept this faith as his strength in difficult times. In youth he was prone to illness and fever brought on by what is not known. Alfred did not allow it to diminish his activity towards the welfare of the people of his realm. He visited a church in Cornwall and prayed and gave alms in silence, beseeching the Lord to take away all his pains. He arose to the amazement of all his pains eliminated and he was cured. Pope Marinus recognized Alfred the Great's devotion to Christianity and bringing it to his people and thus he released the tribute and tax due from the Englishmen. The Pope also showed his friendship by giving him a small piece of the Holy Cross, upon which Jesus Christ had suffered and died for all mankind.

Alfred adopted the idea that learning was the qualification for obtaining positions of responsibility. He was most interested in the qualities necessary to lead the souls of men to Christianity and justice both in harmony with each other. It was a requirement of his children and court officials to learn how to read and become knowledgeable in different subjects in order to rise to more responsible positions within the kingdom. Alfred would read books he thought were important both spiritually and intellectually and then translate them into his own books to be read by others. Four books were amongst these: Gregory's "Pastoral Care", Boethius' "Consolation of Philosophy", and "Orosius" and Bede's "Ecclesiastical History of the English Nation". Alfred during his translations would add his own passages in a way of clarifying in his own right what was being presented to the reader. It would seem he wanted to supply more answers to the subject than was brought forth by the original author who wrote a magnificent book paralleled by none. Alfred qualified his books by identifying with the anguishes against foreign enemies and the pursuit of divine knowledge. These translations show his religious devotion, his own thoughts, and his passion to help others learn through the language of the English.

Alfred sought also to maintain social order, and to do this he created a law-code for each citizen to follow. The law-codes contain his own legislation as well as the books of the Old and New Testament. These laws were found necessary to unify the English people and to create a justice system to bind each person and region together. These laws may have played a substantial role in what would become an epic story between two adversaries, Hereward and the Norman's under William the Conqueror. The excerpts here show

how Hereward could have used the justice system of Alfred, which was overwhelmingly upon his side in this struggle.

> [*Feuds: 42*] *"The man who knows his foe to be sitting at home is not to fight before he asks right of him. If thy foe flees to a church, it is then to be dealt with according to the holiness of that church, as before said. A man may fight on behalf of his born kinsman, if a man attacks him wrongfully, except with his lord: that we do not allow."*

There was, as has been shown, a friendship amongst the Anglo-Saxons and the Frankish kingdom as many marriages were joined between family members in each royal household. Egbert I married the Frankish Princess Redburga, Egbert III married Redburh, possible daughter of Charlemagne, and Alfred the Great's father married Judith, daughter of Charles the Bald. Other connections between the three lineages of Charlemagne will also be found in the story of Hereward.

The legend of Hereward of Bourne in Lincolnshire, also known as Hereward the Wake, is a story of a heroic knight who fights against tremendous odds to free his kinsmen from oppression and wins the admiration of one of the most formidable leaders of his age. The stages of his life went from freeman to oppression and seclusion to military leader with spiritual guidelines. The role played by Hereward during his lifetime would closely mirror those of King Arthur who lived, fought, and died for his land and his people. The similarities between Arthur and Hereward are found by each fighting against an invading army, having loyal knights by their side, abandoned by allies abroad, seeking advice from men of high stature who could be seen as their rivals at the same time, being brave knights willing to risk all to save their land and unify the people, and each of these knight's fate would be lost in history.

The Norman invasion in 1066 by Duke William of Normandy (William the Conqueror) was a devastating time for the Anglo-Saxon people including the nobility. The loss of the Battle of Hastings and the death of King Harold would be the beginning of a great struggle between the two races. Massacres, atrocities, murders, and taking away of lands at the same time putting them into the hands of Norman nobility followed up a full-scale invasion. All these would effect Hereward tremendously as his kinsmen were murdered, including his brother while his lands were also taken. He owned lands in many areas and his father, Leofric, descendant of Alfred the Great, was Earl of Mercia and a possible successor to the Crown. Hereward's early years would be spent preparing him for the struggle he would face later against the Norman aggression.

One item that binds Duke William of Normandy and Hereward together to this day is the Domesday books that were started in 1065 and ended in

1086. These volumes contained all the possessions and values of estates within the kingdom. The records show ownership before the Normans arrived, ownership after it had been transferred, and the actual owner at the last inquiring date. The purpose of these records was for William to see exactly what he had given to his followers and who had seized things without his permission. Principal landowner and tenants are named as well as those lower in social order in great accuracy. The confiscation of land can be examined through these texts and every Norman that acquired land had to obtain approval from a network of justices all the way to the king for it to be upheld. Hereward is shown to have owned land in these records around Bourne, Lincolnshire and also in Warwickshire.

Hereward was the son of Leofric, Earl of Mercia, a nobleman who required discipline and faithful practice to Christianity while being in the court of King Edward the Confessor. Leofric, being of the court, must have provided time for Hereward to gain some favor with the king for he was of high spirits and athletic build. However, he was also undisciplined, unruly and tended to show ambivalence toward the clergy. At the young age of fifteen he was sent out of the country by noble authority to Flanders as had several others with the same issues within court. His livelihood while in Flanders was amongst other nobles including Flemish nobles with the main diet of sport and developing his strength and skills at arms. For this was all Hereward really felt he could master and make proper use of in the future. The time away from his homeland would allow him to gain new surroundings, create new fellowships, and spend more leisure time leading to many acquaintances.

During Hereward's stay in Flanders he would meet two important people in his life, the future wife Torfrida and Baldwin V. Both would be influential in advising Hereward on his future course of actions. Torfrida was a noblewoman who was reverent to liberal knowledge and the mysteries of nature. They were both enchanted with each other and would complement each other in future successes. Baldwin V would offer a different type of counseling which would play an integral role in the struggle between Hereward and King William. This would come in some form of political, religious, and military counseling.

A clear understanding of the connection between the Baldwins, Plantagenets, Normans, Arundells, and Hereward will shed some light on the forces joined before and after the Battle of Hastings. The lineage of Baldwin V of Flander's and Hereward both go back to Alfred the Great, of which each could identify with their ancestral base. However, there was one other major point in that the daughter of Baldwin V was Matilda, who married Duke William of Normandy. This brought Hereward at odds in seeking counsel about possible actions towards events in England. Then there is Godfrey I, Duke of Brabant, Count of Louvain, Duke of Lower Lorraine, the father of

Adeliza of Louvainia, who struggled within the region of Belgium against the Emperors of Germany and sought counsel and help through the aid of Baldwin V in like manner. This is the connection between the future House of Arundell and the future House of Howard. Godfrey II had another daughter named Ida whose marriage to Eustace II produced a son named Eustace III. The latter is named as the one who took King Harold's life and reign to an end during the Battle of Hastings. More importantly, he has family connections between the Plantagenets and the King of Jerusalem. His brother was Godfrey, King of Jerusalem during the first Crusade and cousin of Baldwin II King of Jerusalem. Baldwin II brought together the marriage of his daughter and Fulk V, King of Jerusalem and father of the first Plantagenet Geoffrey V. Thus the Plantagenets and Hereward are joined against the Normans by historical events. Godfrey II and his descendants have a weak alliance with the Normans only by the marriage between Adeliza and William d' Pincerna Albini. The Baldwins seemed to have been allied with each as if a guide to the spiritual with regional concerns in relation to Christianity.

The Battle of Hastings occurred while Hereward was in Flanders in 1066 and at some point after the invasion occurred Hereward decided to visit his family in Bourne in 1069. He would find out during a scouting mission that his brother had been murdered defending his mother and family treasures. Upon learning of this he put on his armor with sword in hand and traveled directly to his besieged home. His arrival was met with the sounds of merry men drinking wine and ale and a stunning discovery of his brother who was beheaded. Hereward in short time ended the lives of all who dwelt on his land and home and afterwards gathered forty-nine men, family members, and friends then proceeded to clear out the Normans from the neighboring lands. A small army began to develop as men heard of what transpired and gained hope from it of regaining their lands. Hereward decided in order to lead this army he must gain recognition, becoming a leader that would clear him of any fault found in him later. A noble abbot, Brant, and monk Wilton of Ely, knighted him in the Abbey of Burgh (Peterborough) with his companions. Hereward found valor in this type of knighting. He perceived it as being nobler to receive a sword and belt from a man of God, for the fittest man to consecrate the soldier of an earthly king is the soldier of Christ.

Recognition of Hereward and his men would come quickly as he drew attention to his military skills and battle readiness by killing the family member of a Norman who was Earl of Surrey, William Warrenne. An alliance with the Danes would next be used to stage a political and religious victory against King William and his abbot at Peterborough. Peterborough dates back to 656, built by Penda, King of Mercia, but was destroyed later by the Danes in 870. It was rebuilt in 971 with enormous recessed arches, vaulted aisles, and painted ceiling. The outside piers were massive in appearance giving it a grandeur of its own, which in turn may be the cause of attacks upon it by the Danes and perhaps the reason for its importance in religious matters during the Norman invasion. The knights seized all the religious remnants of the abbot and charged they were now in the rightful hands of the people of England. The Danes would be of no help from this point on as they defected back to the homeland. Hereward made his way to the Isle of Ely and set up fortification known as Camp of Refuge. A stand was made here by his followers numbering about four thousand not far from Duke William of Normandy's castle in Cambridge. The military experience Hereward gathered in Flanders would surely help him develop strategy to win a certain degree of victory in battle over the Normans. His training gave him the necessary skills to become when needed a great battlefield commander with skills and tactics using infantry and cavalry.

A fortification was built in the Isle of Ely in 1070 from which Hereward would conduct defensive type warfare including raids and blockades against the Normans. This had great effect for a time period with the backing of the local monks, but when the monks were persuaded to stop aiding the revolt King William devised a plan of surrounding the fortification and building a bridge to its walls leaving no avenue of escape. Thousands were killed within the fortification and others were captured and imprisoned while Hereward was able to escape into the ancient forest of Bruneswald. This was his new base for staging attacks against shires in the area of the Abbey of Peterborough. Although gains were made in part by the capture of large estates, Hereward found an opportunity to make piece with King William, who came to admire Hereward's valor and determination. His lands were eventually restored to him by acknowledgment of King William's authority. Around 1086 Hereward was remarried to his new wife Aelfthryth, a noblewoman of great wealth and estate in Worcestershire. This marriage would give him his main line of children as well as position and lands that he fought so long to obtain and were rightfully his. The knight from Bourne had served his countrymen well and gained the admiration he so justly deserved with the rewards he sought in his youth before exile in Flanders.

Robert (Hereward) Howard of Terrington, Norfolk would claim his descent by Hereward and grant land in his name to the church at Lyn. Thus the lineage of Howard began from a legend of England who lived with great honor and won the admiration of both the king and his kinsmen. The positions and peerage of the Howard lineage is extensive and shows that the honor that Hereward lived by was transferred and upheld by his descendants. The following shows how extensive and includes in order held: Knight, Justice of the Common Place, Duke of Norfolk, Admiral of the Navy, Lord, Queen of England, Saint, Earl of Arundell, Baron, and Count. The Howards used their status and abilities in law and warfare to rise to the noble levels they achieved in the fifteenth century and beyond.

William Howard was the great -great grandson of Hereward and the Howard' of the Norfolk line. He lived between 1216-1308 and was a member of the House of Commons of which Edward I had created along with the House of Lords. As Justice of the Common Place he held the highest position attained by the Howard line at that time. His service and honor in this position would bring the Howards into prominence and with their legendary ancestor, Hereward, supported their position in military means as well. William was from East Winch in the area of North Norfolk, the site of the perpendicular church of All Saints. William Howard became Justice of the Common Place and knight in 1297 and he used the revenue from this position to purchase land in East Winch and also became counsel to King's Lynn Corporation a flourishing port area. His career in Parliament would bring his family to new heights and grand marriages bestowing the honors once achieved by Leofric Earl of Mercia.

The first grand marriage would be William's son John Howard I, who would make marriage vows with the great Plantagenet family of England. His marriage was with Joan de Plantagenet de Cornwall, the daughter of Richard de Plantagenet de Cornwall the "King of the Romans" (Holy Roman Emperor). John Howard I became the most important landowner in the area with East Winch, after that of the owners of Castle Rising, a castle built in 1100 AD during the era of Henry I. This marriage may have been joined for reasons of mutual ideas in Christianity and defense of England but most importantly the legendary name it drew upon from the past. John Howard I was most notable in battle in defense of Edward II and becoming Sheriff of Norfolk and Governor of Norwich. These two would establish the Howards in the royal court, the military in defense of the Crown, and the Norfolk region.

John Howard II was accepted in the King's Household due to his mother being of Plantagenet lineage and would also become the Admiral in the Navy in 1335, a prominent position in the kingdom of England due to the always-possible attack from abroad onto its shores. It would also be a significant position in that Alfred the Great created the first known navy in England. Other Howard descendants would also obtain most notable positions, which covered over three hundred years of naval expertise down to Lord Effingham during the Spanish Armada in 1587. John assumed the position of naval engagements against the French coast under Edward III during the Hundred Years War. He presented the Howard arms at East Winch Church sometime before his death in 1388. The Howard lineage had always maintained a Christian and military background as their arms acclaim.

John Howard III would increase the already enlarging estates of the family during three marriages, ending with Alice Tendering. The three marriages yielded estates in Essex, Hertfordshire, and Cambridgeshire and finally the new chief seat Tendering Hall, Stoke by Nayland in Suffolk. He continued the military services of the family in the navy as Admiral of the Northern Seas until his death in Jerusalem in 1437 during pilgrimage there.

The second grand marriage was between Robert Howard and Margaret Mowbray, who was the daughter of Thomas Mowbray the great-great-grandson of Edward I. The Mowbray's had risen to the Duke of Norfolk until Thomas was banished by Richard II to Venice where he died. When Thomas Mowbray, Duke of Norfolk, died the title and the estates passed to his daughter who then passed it onto her husband and the Howard family. John Howard the son of Robert would thus become the first Duke of Norfolk (the third creation) by marriage. John was very distinguished amongst his peerage, especially the Plantagenets, as he sided with the Yorkist as did succeeding Howards until 1485 upon Richard III death. He gained the support of Edward IV of England for his part in the battle of St. Alban's. John was made a Knight, Constable of Norwich Castle, Sheriff of Norfolk and Suffolk, and Treasurer of the Royal Household for his continued support of Richard III Plantagenet during the disposition of Edward V in 1483. Other honours bestowed for this allegiance were Earl Marshal of England and Lord Admiral of all England, Ireland, and Aquitaine. A new creation was given to him on 1467 making him Lord Howard and envoy to France, where he took part in meetings of troop withdrawals between Edward IV and Louis XI. John Howard became the rightful owner of Framlingham Castle upon Lady Mowbray's death. The castle and the title of Duke of Norfolk were the establishment of the royal household of the Howard Lineage since it began with Robert (Hereward) Howard.

One of the major battles won by John Howard was as a King's Lieutenant and Captain during the Anglo-Scottish War as commander of the English fleet and the *Mary Howard* ship. The Scottish fleet was either burnt or captured, giving England its first major naval victory. His death would come in 1485 defending Richard III in battle at Bosworth Field against the troops of Henry VII as commander of the military during the closing of the War of the Roses. This battle was doomed to fail on Richard III's side from the outset, for amongst his troops were defectors from his cause of which John Howard must not have been aware or have much concern over. Once the battle started the army under John broke through the main lines only to have a good portion of his army fail to uphold the rear, causing him to be surrounded and finally defeated. Richard III was also defeated at Bosworth Field as the Plantagenet line would now decline after five centuries of defending Christianity and their homeland and willing to die for its cause. John Howard was buried as a Duke of Norfolk in Cluniac monastery instead of the family burial at Stoke by Nayland.

Thomas Howard was the second Duke of Norfolk and Lieutenant General of the northern borders with qualities of an able diplomat, soldier, and administrator whose principles would guide him to new heights within the royal court under Edward IV and Henry VIII. More significant in his early years was the time he spent in Europe in the services of the court of Charles the Bold, brother-in-law to Edward IV. The cultural extravagances under Charles were not far from the ideas and tastes of Thomas, who always sought out higher forms of society. A major event after being Knighted in 1478 was being given the honors of carrying the Sword of State at Richard III's coronation. His allegiance to the king would be both rewarding and costly as he would be wounded at Bosworth Field while fighting alongside his father. Thomas Howard was given clemency by Henry VII in return for his services under careful scrutiny until he could be again rewarded the title of Duke of Norfolk in 1507. One of his final tasks was escorting Margaret Tudor to Edinburg for the marriage ceremonies with James IV of Scotland. This marriage would lead to the reign of James I, the Stuarts. In 1513 under his command the Scottish invasion was halted and left leaderless in defeat, creating such a victory for Thomas Howard that since that day forward he was to be treated in the same manner as a prince of royal blood. The final days of Thomas, whose family seat was Framlingham Castle, Suffolk came in 1524 after which he was given a grand burial ceremony of the age. The significance of the bishop of Ely receiving the body is the historical period four hundred years previous when Hereward held is ground at Ely against Duke William of Normandy after being knighted.

The second Duke of Norfolk would be more notable for being the father of three great lines of the Howard family. These lines would show the Golden Era of the Howard Family who would attain great stature, peerage, wealth, and notability during the sixteenth century. The sixteenth century would be an age of grandeur and turmoil with honorable men who had visions and ideas that would bring prosperity to their people and acceptance of Christianity. The ruling nobility of this time included Charles V (Holy Roman Emperor), Rudolph II (Holy Roman Emperor), Henry VIII (King of England), Elizabeth I (Queen of England). The Howard family was acclaimed for their willingness to do great service for the King, Queen, and Holy Roman Emperor while at the same time doing great service for their faith. The departure to an extreme on the side of the latter would come into question of one's loyalty to the Crown of England.

The first line of Howards from Thomas Howard descends to Charles Howard, first Earl of Nottingham, Lord of Effingham, Knight, Ambassador to France, Lord High Admiral, and Lord Lieutenant General of England. He was cousin of Elizabeth I and would serve the Crown in all aspects of military and political matters. His skills at sea were obtained under his father William Howard, Earl of Effingham, and would become useful under the reign of Elizabeth I during the Spanish Armada in 1587 and again in 1596, which he won a major victory for the Queen. As commissioner at the trial of Queen Mary of Scotland in 1586 and Gunpowder Plot in 1605 Charles showed his political allegiance to the Queen of England.

The second line of Howards from Thomas Howard descends to the third Duke of Norfolk Thomas Howard and Henry Howard both played major roles during the reign of Henry VIII by orchestrating marriages with his nieces to marry the King. These attempts to raise the level of the Howards and the Catholic Church, however, would be seen in a different light by both the Crown and his nobles. Thomas Howard, fourth Duke of Norfolk, was known for his great marriages he had between prominent nobles. These were in order Mary Fitz-Alan, heiress to Earl of Arundell, Margaret Audley, heiress to Baron of Walden, Elizabeth Leyburne, widow of Thomas Dacre, Baron of Gillesland. Thomas' sons would marry his wife's three daughters making their surname D' Acre-Howard. The surname D'acre comes form De (from) Acre (city in Israel) of which the line was born. His last attempted marriage was with Mary Queen of Scots, for which he would be executed.

The fourth Duke of Norfolk' son Philip Howard inherited the Earl of Arundell and would become in great turmoil with Elizabeth I for his Catholic devotion. Philip was baptized at Whitehall Palace with the Royal Family in attendance along with is his godfather King Philip II of Spain after who he was named. The fact that he was second cousin to the Elizabeth I and Catholic was a very precarious position while at the same time being dutiful to Philip II of Spain under Catholic rule. Sometime around the Spanish Armada previously spoken of Philip Howard attempted to leave for Spain, for an unknown reason, but was brought back by the Queen and imprisoned in the Tower of London in 1585. There he would die without proof of guilt upon which he was buried below Arundell Castle. Pope Paul VI canonized him in 1970 as one of forty martyrs of England and Wales.

Thomas Howard Earl of Arundell was the son Philip had never seen while imprisoned in the Tower of London. A very accomplished nobleman he traveled abroad to be educated in France, Rome, Camps of the Low Countries, and Universities such as St. Omers. An illness brought him to Padua, Italy to recover and he became impressed by its magnificent artwork and culture. He made a return visit which included Venice, Padua, Florence, Siena, Rome, and Naples to look at local art collections. Thomas became a master and had natural disposition in sculptures, design, painting and architecture. He began to collect sculptures as well as have them commissioned by artist she favored thus showing his interest in classical antiquity for honor and nobility showing both order and propriety. In 1621 he began acquiring sculptures from abroad in Greece and Asia Minor through agents who would deal with the obtaining, bargaining, shipping, and politics that came with the endeavor. Among the works he was able to acquire included Cicero, Soldier of Rome, Henry VII, Trojan War frieze, Felix Gem, Venus, Sphinxes, Columns of Apollo, Athena, Wounded Amazon, and his own statue he commissioned. These are all on display now at the University of Oxford Museum, England. He died in Padua, Italy where he lived apart from the civil war in England partaking of the passion he had learned throughout his life.

The last line of Howard's from Thomas Howard descends to the highest peerage that would be obtained in the Court of England. Lord Edmund Howard was his third son and held Lord based on his father being Duke of Norfolk. Edmund however was never a member of the House of Lords as the peerage would show. His daughters on the other hand would marry into nobility bringing them both grandeur and sorrows.

Katherine Howard who lived between 1520-1542 married King Henry VIII and became Queen of England in 1540. The future Queen's grandmother, the Dowager Duchess in Horsham, Norfolk and Lambeth, Surrey, brought her up. Her age was much less than that of Henry VIII when they married in 1540 and her actions were not withstanding his wishes upon the Queen This would lead to Henry VIII falling into disfavor with the Queen leading to her early death not unlike the preceding marriages. Katherine was pretty, intellectual, delightful, and well dressed with clothes from France and Henry VIII considered her "a rose without a thorn". The opposition to the marriage induced the King under certain events to become intolerant to the shortcomings of Queen Katherine, leading the Crown to hand down the same judgment as his preceding wives had received. Katherine never left her faith and held to Christian doctrine until the day of her death.

Margaret Howard, sister to Katherine, would marry Sir Thomas Arundell whose lineage went back to Adeliza Queen of England. The joining of these two family lines was equal if not more magnificent as the one between the Howards and the Plantagenets. Thomas Arundell would bring to the marriage his ancestral name handed down by Adeliza "Countess Arundell" and her husband William Pincerna d" Albini who inherited Arundell Castle. Thomas Arundell had extraordinary amounts of lands, manors he inherited from his father Sir John Arundell X, and others granted to him by Henry VIII. They were an extensive amount of property. Margaret Howard was also granted an extensive amount of land and manors by Henry VIII upon the death of Katherine, which combined with Thomas Arundell created enormous wealth for the family. Furthermore, Thomas Arundell added even greater prominence in the purchase of Wardour Castle, inherited by Margaret after his death. This great wealth would come at a price later under the Crown of Elizabeth I. Wardour Castle would become renowned for its owner by Margaret Howard's grandson Baron Thomas Arundell of Wardour. The marriage between these two Catholic families deep rooted in English history with royal lineages would bring forth in future generations remarkable duties for their faith, country, and family beginning a new precedence of the time.

The Howard lineage was renowned for its resilience in battle, adherence to the Catholic faith, and the peerage it held for the better good of all Englishmen. As Yeatman has documented, in the past no family has held more peerage or higher peerage as that of the Howards. The Duke of Norfolk was actually a claim of representation in honor of the ancient Dukes of Normandy represented by the House of Albini, Earls of Arundell and Mowbray, Dukes of Norfolk. From Alfred the Great to Hereward of Bourne and then to Queen Katherine Howard there was a continuous struggle for both faith and England.

VII

ARUNDELL

Eloquent in council and bold in action, this nobleman was respected by his contemporaries, both as a statesman and as a soldier, his prudence enabled him to steer wide of the difficulties which involved so many others of his day in ruin, and his moderation always secured him to the esteem even of those to whom he was opposed.

William d' Albini, Earl of Arundell, "The Early Genealogical History of the House of Arundell" Tierney 287

THE THIRD ROYAL LINEAGE that was descendant of Charlemagne was the House of Arundell. Their lineage goes back to the Holy Roman Emperors who succeeded Charlemagne and to the area where the Franks began in Northern Europe around Belgium (Belgica), the ancestors of Adeliza of Louvania, Queen of England. On the other side of the Arundell Lineage the ancestral line began in Normandy (France) in the region of St. Sauvuer, the ancestors of William Pincerna d' Albini and where Duke William of Normandy and his ancestors had become rulers of a Duchy. The history of the Arundell line would be more intriguing than turbulent and although it would lose its peerage over time it would not lose the great name attached to it. The surname of Arundell is deep-rooted in ancient Norman history with ties to the Franks and Normans. They were the cornerstones of medieval Europe and controlled most of the land and coast of Western Europe and England from 700 – 1200 AD. Their strength was drawn by what had already been accomplished by the Frankish King Clovis the Great and Charles the Great, Charlemagne.

This royal family lineage picks up from the Frankish lineage and its turmoil between father and son, both Holy Roman Emperors, Louis "The Pious" and Lothar I, which would end in a break up of the Holy Roman Empire initially by three parts. This breakup would only be the beginning as the Western Empire slowly would fragment into areas held by kings and under them vassals of land held by Dukes and Counts. The Holy Roman Emperor would have a designated region he was from and maintained control over the entire Empire. This would change over time due to power issues between the kings and the Holy Roman Emperor as to who it was rightfully designated, by hereditary means or by the Pope.

Flanders-Belgium would maintain great wealth along with political and religious strength after the decline of the Carolingian Dynasty. This was mainly due to its location, ancestral ties of the past, and a great family like the Baldwins who were linked to the Kingship of Jerusalem. Major cities in the region developed and linked to older cities of the past including Aachen (Germany), Lorraine (France), Louvain, Hainualt, and Brabrant. This was the area where Clovis and Charlemagne spent most of their days in battle, assemblies, or leisure. A Royal family of Dukes and Counts began to emerge with ties to the Baldwins, Normans, and King of Jerusalem.

Godfrey I became the most proclaimed descendant after Lothar I as he was both Duke and Count of many regions. Godfrey I (1060 – January, 25 1139) called the Bearded, the Courageous, or the Great, was the landgrave of Brabant, and count of Brussels and Leuven (or Louvain) from 1095 to his death and Duke of Lower Lorraine from 1106 to 1129. He was also Margrave of Antwerp from 1106 to his death.

Godfrey I was known for his action against the Holy Roman Emperors of his time. He first came into conflict with Otbert, Bishop of Liège, over the county of Brunengeruz that both claimed. In 1099, Emperor Henry IV allotted the county to the bishop, who entrusted it in turn to Albert III, Count of Namur. Godfrey was in favour with the Emperor Henry IV and defended his interests in Lorraine. Godfrey I stopped Robert II of Flanders in 1102 from invading the Cambraisis. After the death of the Emperor in 1106, his son and successor, Henry V began to avenge himself on his father's partisans. Duke Henry of Lower Lorraine was imprisoned and his duchy confiscated and given to Godfrey I. Henry escaped from prison and attempted to retake his duchy by capturing Aachen, which ultimately failed. In 1114, during a rift between Henry V and Pope Paschal II, Godfrey I led a revolt in Germany. Both parties came to terms in 1118 as the Emperor and the Duke were reconciled.

Henry V died in 1125 and Godfrey I supported Conrad of Hohenstaufen, the Duke of Franconia, against Lothair of Supplinburg. Lothair was elected. Lothair withdrew the Duchy of Lower Lorraine and granted it to Waleran, the son of Henry, whom Henry V had deprived in 1106. Godfrey maintained the Margraviate of Antwerp and retained the Ducal title known as Duke of Brabant established in 1183. Godfrey spent his last years in the abbey of Affligem and died of old age. Godfrey I had a royal bloodline from the Holy

Roman Emperors, sons of Charlemagne, which would allow his children to marry into similar royal families from England and Jerusalem.

The first daughter of Godfrey I, Ida, married Eustace II, the brother of Godfrey King of Jerusalem and whose son Eustace III was named for ending the reign of King Harold at Hastings. Eustace II was also cousin to Baldwin II King of Jerusalem. The most notable daughter was Adeliza of Louvania, a very beautiful and aristocratic lady who married the King of England Henry I and became Queen consort from 1121-1135. Their difference in age was about forty years but the main reason for the marriage may have been her royal lineage along with the possibility of a male heir of which Henry I wanted to secure before his death. During the fifteen years of marriage there still was not a male heir born to Henry I who died in 1135. The consequence of this lack of heir was a designation of the Crown of England to Stephen, leaving Adeliza as a Dowager Queen of England and "Countess of Arundell". William the Conqueror had two successors in William II and Henry I, both controlled who built castles in the English kingdom, but when Henry I died he left a female heir in Matilda of which no woman ever held the Crown of England. Stephen of Blois, her cousin, would claim the Crown in her place only to hand it over at his death to Geoffrey V Plantagenet and thus the beginning of the Plantagenet Kings of England.

Adeliza was an elegant and pretty Dowager Queen of England who would find her new love after a time of mourning at the monastery in William Pincerna d' Albini, first Earl of Arundell, chief advisor to Henry I. They would come to live very happy lives with the inheritance from Henry I, including the Norman castles of Arundell, Sussex, and Castle Rising. Adeliza was very active in church affairs and gave property to Reading Abbey and other foundation in her former husband name. Her stay in the royal residence of Arundell was the future residence of all Earls of Arundell since 1151 when she left to spend her final years at the Abbey of Affligem, Brabant and later buried by her father Godfrey I. Adeliza's life was of storybook quality in relation to her father, Henry I, stepmother Matilda, and William d' Pincerna Albini whose descendants would bear the name of Arundell from where he served and lived in grandeur with his fair wife.

Royal beginnings of Albini, St. Sauvuer, the Contentin, and the Dukes of Normandy must be explored to understand how the royal bloodline of Arundell was established before the time of William d' Albini. The Dukes of Normandy began with Rollo, of Frankish-Scandinavian origin. Charles the Simple in the Treaty of St. Clair-sur-Epte granted Rollo in 911 land in the upper eastern part of Normandy. The lower parts of Normandy were granted later, which made a duchy for the new Duke in what once had been Frankish lands. The land was granted in three time periods 911, 924, and 933 including land of the Contentin and lands that once belonged to the Romans. Over time the duchy of the upper part of Normandy became more French (Frankish) while the lower part remained Scandinavian by the invading peoples. This issue would split the populace of the region and cause rebellions throughout to see who would eventually rule over the Ducal House.

The Normans had now become a Scandinavian held territory with remnants of ancient Roman and Gaul of which the lands extended into. Their hold on the region came from the count (*comtes*) and viscount (*viscomtes*) status they held when granted the land by the Franks. These were a people with many qualities including seamanship, adventurous, dynamic, energetic, and powerful in entering into new lands and taking them into their own system of governing such as England in 1066. Upon their arrival to Normandy and many decades after they increasingly accepted the Frankish religion, customs, organization, warfare and learning criteria. The Frankish-Scandinavian integration in Normandy would make its people one of the most predominant and powerful of duchies on the European Continent.

Dukes of Normandy were both strong and fierce in battles from which the male line descended from the first Duke of Normandy Rollo. His descendants from 911 to 1045 were William I (Guillaume), Richard I "The Fearless", Richard II "The Good", Richard III, his brother Robert I, and then his son William the Conqueror. Their system of governing was feudalism, knight's service in the fiefs, and castle building within the fiefs. Knighthood was started very early in life and each was to learn the ways of the cavalry. The knights were expected to serve the Duke in many regions such as Spain, Italy, and England. These were the people within Normandy who held the ruling class and served their lord in his honor and in the Frankish custom. They also drew their power from the Latin-Christian church adopted upon the baptism of Rollo, giving them a more civilized side to the knightly ferocity in battle. During the time of William "The Conqueror" many religious buildings in Normandy were erected including Tosny, Beaumount, Montgomery, and St. Sauvuer of the Contentin. These Normans had a religious zeal and each would have monks within their church for religious teachings that were highly looked upon for the ruling class of barons, counts, and viscounts below the Duke.

The most distinguished family in the ninth and tenth centuries during the rise of the Normans were the knights, barons, and viscounts of St. Sauvuer in the Contentin. They had won favor for their knightly achievement during the time of Rollo, first Duke of Normandy in 933. Their status increased over time until 1045 when William d' Albini became Pincerna of the royal household. His ancestors and their royal position are Richard I St. Sauvuer (baron), Nigel St. Sauvuer (Neil I, baron), Roger St. Sauvuer, Nigel St. Sauvuer (Neil II, baron), Nigel St. Sauvuer (Neil III, viscount). A marriage between Richard III, Duke of Normandy's daughter Helena to Nigel St. Sauvuer (Neil II) in about 1020 could be assumed to be the reason for their political rise within the royal household.

William Pincerna d' Albini's father was Nigel St. Sauvuer (Neil III) who was a viscount during the time of William the Conqueror and his battles against rebellion from those seeking to obtain the Dukedom in regard to what they considered higher status and more worthy of the title. In 1047 William gained full support from within Normandy after his victory at Val-es-Dunes at Caen defeating rivals to the throne Reginald I, Burgundy, and his son Gui of Brionne with the aid of Henry I King of France. The battle was won against an army of 25,0000, a mere fraction of that of the army of Duke William. Nigel St. Sauvuer (Neil III) was probably in some capacity at the aid of Duke William during the battle and gained favor since he became viscount and his son gained a high position of Pincerna soon after. Duke William's victories would bring cohesiveness to both upper and lower Normandy and consolidate his effort in 1053 when his main rivals of Henry I King of France and Geoffrey V Plantagenet had passed away. He would introduce the Truce of God supported by the Pope in his Christian mission across the Channel into England.

The justice system in Normandy was aided by Duke William's viscounts who had the authority to uphold judicial law, financial issues, military necessities, administrative duties, and the building of castles. These viscounts throughout Normandy, such as Nigel St. Sauvuer (Neil III), helped to resolve governmental problems within the duchy allowing Duke William to concentrate on greater events affecting it internally and externally. The Duke would now set his knights and military might to the English Kingdom by papal blessing to reform the English Church in what could be considered a Christian war against the Anglo-Saxons.

The Norman invasion of England was a successful military campaign in 1066 which was orchestrated by attacking with three marching earldoms against the existing earldoms of the Anglo-Saxons and other regions including Wales, Chester, Shrewsbury, Hereford, Kent, and Cornwall as well as to the north in East Anglia and Northumbria. Castles were built establishing military positions in each region of Hastings, Pevensey, Lewes, Chichester, Richmond, and Arundell under the possession of Roger Montgomery. Nigel St. Sauvuer's (Neil III) grandson Nigel of Avaranches, known as Robert, was made the constable of a high military rank and officer of the state in Chester. In 1077 he fought against the Welsh at the battle of Ruddlan and was made the first baron of Halton were he built a motte-and-bailey castle on Halton Hill in Northwest Cheshire, Wales. This was the seat of the barons from the eleventh century to the fourteenth century until it passed to the Duchy of Lancaster during the reign of King Henry IV. The motte-and-bailey castle was the style used throughout France, Normandy, and England during the eleventh century. A small hill would be built up and topped by a wooden or stone structure "keep". A motte was built around the hill with a large courtyard of baileys surrounded by wooden fences. The use of earldoms, the castles built on them, and the counts and barons to administer and defend them were the Norman's success in England. The success in Wales by Nigel of Avranches (Robert) would not go unforeseen by William, Duke of Normandy because he would become Baron and Lord of the northern lands of Wales. His cousin William d' Albini would be present with Duke William at Hastings as Pincerna to the royal household.

William Pincerna d' Albini's life was one any nobleman would wish to have attained. His life would have a foundation of a royal bloodline and forged by the traits of valor as a soldier, moderator, respected by the religious order and bishops, and Earl of Arundell. William d' Albini served three Kings of England and the Queen of England giving him a reputation of great duty and trust among the nobility in the eleventh and twelve centuries. He maintained his standing by being honorable and righteous during times of difficulty and unrest within the kingdom and the court. To understand the life of William d' Albini one must first start with his royal ancestry, the foundation for all the great services and positions he held.

The history of the name of Albini is deep rooted into the region of France and Normandy. The name has many spellings including Aubigny, Aubini, and finally the one related to the French spelling of Albini. These names have been traced back to the records obtained from St. Alban's from which they became benefactors of after the Norman conquests of England. The position of Pincerna is known to be the office of state held by the Albinis at the time of King Canute of England brought by Princess Emma of Normandy. This was the highest office of state in both England and Normandy and it is possible that the Albinis moved from one region to the next as they were needed. There was only one position of Pincerna in both regions and it was probably established about thirty years before Emma coming to England from Normandy in 1030. William d' Albini accompanied William the Conqueror to England in 1045 and was in full military armor in the battle of Val es Dunes. This establishes the ancestry was from Normandy and further records show that they were connected to the church of St. Sauvuer.

The chapel of St. Sauvuer is connected with two noble houses in France. The first is by Richard the Dane, Viscount of the Contentin, who founded the chapel in St. Sauvuer in 913. The chapel was enlarged by Roger de St. Sauvuer his grandson and after that his son Neil II St. Sauvuer, who turned it into a monastery. The next mention is in relation to grants of churches in Guernsey by Duke William to Nigel (Niel III St. Sauvuer) in 1060. There is good reason to believe that the Albinis (St. Sauvuer) were also the Viscount of the Contentin in France as well but since they had left France it was forfeited to the Eudes until their return. Thus the name is inherited from the two chapels St. Sauvuer, France and St. Albans, England. The name of St. Sauvuer can be traced back to Robert I, King of France and then to Charlemagne, Holy Roman Emperor.

William Pincerna d' Albini was gifted in many ways, gaining him many honors and social prestige. Before his romance and preceding marriage with Adeliza he was also romantically involved with the Queen of France. The latter would be only a passing romance while the former would lead to many children. He made struggles that would have come down to great losses including many lives into great rewards, making life for those in England better. One matter was an issue with Stephen, then King of England when he invited Adeliza to Arundell Castle, the base of operations at the time, to show his hospitality. This did not go well with Stephen who thought it was a matter of treason to the King in an attempt to take the Crown from him. William d' Albini was quickly restored since Stephen had more pressing matters to attend. Henry II Plantagenet had arrived in England seeking the Crown considered rightfully his. The nobility of England and Scotland was on Henry II's side as they met with full military armor to settle the right to the Crown. William d" Albini, Earl of Chichester, seeing an infantry such as Henry II's could not be defeated, sought righteousness by giving his honest opinion on the battle ensuing. He persuaded Stephen that no justice could be done through battle that was decisively against him. The wiser William, winning a victory for both sides, adverted losses in battle while at the same time seeking unity among the nobility. The trait of temperance over possible victory would sustain him over his great courage. He would later in life be given the Earldom of Arundell and Sussex gaining him the leadership of the nobility. All the Arundells who have descended from William Pincerna d' Albini would seek to portray the same traits of courage, virtue, and piety.

Arundell Castle overlooks the river Arun in West Sussex, England, the grandest castle made for the Royal residence since being granted to Roger de Montgomery in 1077 by Duke William the Norman. Henry II gave William d' Albini the Castle and the Earldom of Arundell as King of England in respect to his marriage with Adeliza. The Dukes of Norfolk would also hold the Castle of Arundell under the Howards from the fifteenth to the seventeenth century while withstanding the War of the Roses and the Civil War. The builders of Arundell Castle were before Norman times and it was only after the invasion when updates had begun by the Normans with their own architecture. The earlier builders were most likely from Gaelic or Belgic districts of Soissons from which the name of Sussex is derived. These people lived on the land way before the Romans came and the stones used to build the Castle are from the Plain of Salisbury the same place the Stonehenge stones were taken.

Arundell is determined to have derived from the ancient Gaelic word for Dale or Valley of the Water. An area around the Castle is in a valley causing flooding during times of heavy rain into the Arun River. The early lords of the area were thus called Kings of Arundell. The Earl of Arundell title did not begin until William d' Albini after the Norman invasion. The name *Arundell* was adopted before the time of Edward the Confessor (1042 –1066) by all who lived within its castle walls. However, there are other known meanings to the word as adopted through the generations. The Gualish word for *arond* is "swallow" which is the arms used all the way back to the Kings of Sussex. Another terminology for the word is the traits of the users to be gallant in action and prompt in expedition. It would be safe to say that the name is derived from the same source but used to signify different things such as the land, the animals, and traits of its inhabitants.

There are four great Houses that are derived from the House of Albini and are Duke of Norfolk, Duke of Rutland, Arundells of Cornwall, and Percival. The Duke of Norfolk is descended from Mowbray, a descendant from Nigel (Neil), granted to him by Henry I who is also the grandson of William d' Albini. The Duke of Rutland is from the Ducal House of Belvoir held by William d' Albini who was the hero at the battle of Tinchebrai. The House of Arundell has a direct male line to this day from the first Earl of Arundell, William Pincerna d' Albini, although not all were considered to be the Earl of Arundell. Earl of Arundell was the creation, like the Duke of Norfolk by Henry I. House of Percival comes from the Ducal House of Brittany while the other Houses have lineage to the Ducal House of Normandy by Albini and St. Sauvuer. The Albinis who were the Viscount of the Contentin ceded by the King of France to Rollo, Duke of Normandy in 912, passed to Robert I and then Richard I are the ancestors of St. Sauvuer.

Origins of the Titles given were established before the Norman period in the same manner as the Franks had chosen theirs. The meaning of Earl and Count are synonymous but do have one true difference. An Earl is a secondary to the Prince, "next" Prince, or Chief. Therefore, an Earl does not necessarily have territory if he is next in succession to the reigning Prince. A Count is one who rules a territory and need not be a Prince if the territory is of a large nature (shire) thus he becomes as Earl by default. An Earl was created by personal dignity at birth while Count was a created office. A Count and even an Earl having territory would be allowed to take a share in the profits of the county he was from, the other part going to the King. This situation led to many Earls actually being given territory instead of only holding Title. The Earl of Arundell is also Earl of Sussex, enjoying the profits of his county of Sussex. These Titles were also given in being faithful to the King in time of any crisis that may arise within the kingdom or the respective county. A shire or county is from the Gaelic word *tshir* meaning land, a territory the early inhabitants established for themselves with names that are distinct to the traits of the people originally establishing the county. It must be noted that an Earldom in some cases if separate in government such as may have been the case in Cornwall at some time period, can be considered a Duchy. Robert Duke of Normandy used this Title frequently from the use of Earl. This is how the titles are distinguished within the royal court of the kingdom and is still recognized to this day.

The Title of Earl of Arundell passed through five members of the Albini family until it fell into disuse and passed to the Fitzalan family when Isabel d' Albini married John Fitzalan. The family name then switched to Arundell and would not come into great prominence again until Sir Thomas Arundell in 1485 under Henry VII. Throughout this period the Arundells would acquire many lands, manors, and churches while marrying into predominant families of the time.

A story of one land acquisition has an interesting story line connected to it when Robert de Arundell purchased land within the region of Cornwall. His purchase was in Treloy during the reign of Richard the Lionheart and then John Lackland. The story goes he was hunting within the lands of Cornwall for venison and had come to shoot and take venison for his own. The king heard of what occurred and took it as an offense for venturing to hunt for sport on his own domain. King John took action against William d' Albini II by taking possession of the castle. The said William d' Albini II died and in order for William d' Albini III to regain the castle he had to pay an enormous fine. In all, William d' Albini III paid some 350 marks for recompense of Castle of Pec, Honour of Arundell, and Lancashire.

The Arundells would be known most notably for owning the manor of Lanherne. John Arundell I inherited the manor through his mother's side, who held two parts ownership. Lanherne property can be traced back to the Hundred owned by Richard of Cornwall "King of the Romans". Another grant that goes back to Richard of Cornwall relates to John Arundell III and his marriage to Elizabeth of Carminowe. A grant to her grandfather Roger Carminowe by Richard of Cornwall gave grant to the rights of water to run from the manor of Helston to the mill of Carminowe. Richard of Cornwall was by all means the wealthiest of the European Continent and the brother of King Henry III, and the Arundells who lived in the area of Cornwall came into interchange with the Plantagenets.

The stature of the Arundells is greatly represented by John Arundell VI who was created a Knight of the Bath at the coronation of Henry IV in 1399. He would serve under three Kings of England including Henry V and Henry VI as sheriff of Cornwall. This was the honour to His Majesty to keep the peace in a county of great importance to the kingdom. He served six years at this position and then moved on to greater duties to the King. The Duke of Exeter and Admiral of England Thomas Beaufort made a master of a vessel within the fleet of His Majesty John Arundell VI in 1418. The Beauforts, named after a castle in France, were direct descendants of the Plantagenets by the marriage of John Gaunt, Duke of Lancaster, and Katherine Swynford. The crowning of Richard II was with great ceremony and it was presided over by John Gaunt who was his uncle. He was the leading figure in the government during an unpopular time and had to bear the load for the King. Richard II kept him close by due to his ability to have luck on his side. On the other hand, he despised the Arundells due their heavy-handed ways, tough, aristocratic, and lack of humor in the wake of struggle. Richard II was found to be overly much of what Arundell was not and thus brought his military aides such as Gaunt around to his court while Arundell again sided with Henry IV.

Upon the death of John Arundell VI a vast amount of wealth was distributed attaining to his great services to the King and his inheritances. Amongst these were the manor of Lanhadron, Lanherne, Treloy, St. Columb, and certain dignitaries to the Monastery of St. Michael's Mount in Cornwall. This monastery at the time was related to the Abbey of St. Michael's in the Contentin where the St. Sauvuer family had been benefactors. The long standing ties to Normandy by the Arundell's was finally beginning to decline after five centuries when they were made barons on the Contentin.

The prosperity of the Arundells continued with his son John Arundell VII who was created Vice Admiral of Cornwall in 1447 for the service of His Majesty the King by the Earl of Suffolk. He married first Elizabeth and second Catherine Childioc. By his first wife he left a gentleman's sum to acquaintances adding up to around thirty-two or more manors to hold until the death of his wife Elizabeth. His final grant asked only that she be given one red rose per year in fee. Another deed is to his second wife, granted some twenty manors in all including to his son John Arundell IX and Thomas Arundell, who married Catherine Dinham.

Thomas Arundell would be both attainted by King Richard III and restored by the next reigning King of England, Henry VII, due to his bravery in the battle of Bosworth Field. His services to the later King of England in 1485 in the famous battle for inheritance of the Crown was by what some believe between a pious ruler and one who had fallen from graces due to his actions against his brothers in the Tower. In this battle he would gain knightly status second only in degree to William d' Albini during his services in battle for William, Duke of Normandy and Stephen, King of England. The successes on the battlefield and the bravery shown against a very skilled military such as that of Richard III with his commander John Howard would bestow great honours on the family in the future. His marriage to Catherine also brought him more social regard and manors including the Castle of Wardour.

The next marriage that brought the Arundells into further prominence was between John Arundell X and Elizabeth, the daughter of Sir Thomas Grey, Marquis of Dorset. This allowed the Arundells to have more connection with Henry VIII King of England. The history behind this is the Plantagenet Lineage, which descends in the following manner: Edward III, Edmund of Langley Duke of York, Edward Duke of York, Richard of York and Earl of Cambridge, Richard Duke of York, Edward IV of York, Elizabeth of York (married Henry VII Tudor and son Sir Thomas Grey), and Elizabeth Grey (daughter of Sir Thomas Grey) married John Arundell X. This made Thomas Grey half brother to Henry VIII and Elizabeth Arundell cousin german to Henry VIII. John Arundell X died in 1513 and had two sons John XI and Thomas Arundell who were both given great honors by their father and the Dorset's. A second marriage by John X had a daughter Mary who married Henry Fitz Alan, Earl of Arundell. The wealth and honour bestowed on John Arundell X could be justified by his father's services to the Crown in time of struggles and his great character inherit to the Arundells.

Thomas Arundell was born in 1500 and increased his father's wealth by no less means but yet in more changing times and forces on the people and church of England. He was a man of great intellect and culture who could attain many great things abroad, yet stayed in England to serve the people and the Crown. The stature he obtained, which was significant in many ways, was in testament to the Arundell honor and character. The changes that would be implemented by Henry VIII and the indignities he made upon his court would give Thomas no secure ground in which to make a difference in the downward spiral of the situation of the sixteenth century.

The virtue of Thomas was greatly shown for his work with the Catholic Church and Cardinal Wolsey. He was both a pupil and friend with the Cardinal during a time of change within the church from its old doctrine. King Henry VIII had made himself head of the Church, beginning the struggle between the Crown, Court, and the Catholic priests. During this chain of events Cardinal Wolsey would be replaced by the Henry VIII, in some probability beginning a struggle that would have no just ending.

A marriage could obtain a nobleman four things: more trust within parties, greater allies, property, and a higher position. It just so happens that Thomas Arundell and Henry VIII were two ships heading on a collision that neither could avoid. Thomas would marry Margaret Howard, the daughter of Edmund Howard the second son of the Duke of Norfolk imprisoned by Henry VII for opposing him during the Battle of Bosworth Field. This may not have set well with the King for purposes of alliances. The marriage gave him the right to quarter the arms of many great houses including the Albinis, Fitz Alans (Earls of Arundell), Earl of Chester, and Montgomerys of the House of Childioc. Henry VIII married at the same time Anne Boleyn, who was the niece of the Duke of Norfolk. The indignities done to the Queen and the state of the Church in England had now brought a conflict even closer.

Thomas Arundell, Lord of Wardour's wealth was extensive due to his inheritance from his father John Arundell X, his marriage with Margaret Howard, and his purchase thereafter of Wardour Castle. He was now one of the richest men in England and would later acquire a new title to go with the vast amount of land, manors, and castles. The new purchase of Wardour

Castle would stay in the family for centuries to come. It was built on a land held by Waleran Venator, a knight of high standing and a veteran of the Hundred Years War with France. In the Domesday Book the land was called Wardour and a castle was built later by Lord John Lovel and Holland on the same land in 1393. In 1461 King Edward of York confiscated the castle from the Lancastrian during the War of the Roses. The castle passed hands many times from the Dinham Family, Lord Brooke, and Willoughby and then sold to Thomas Arundell. The castle lies in Wiltshire, England in the countryside beside a lake in a tranquil setting. It was built in the same style of the chateauxs in France with many comforts that were not in earlier castles used for military purposes. The castle was unparalleled in standards by the hexagonal floor plans, flanked by towers to the entrance and a courtyard in the center of the building containing a well. A grand hallway was built above the entrance to the castle leading to the Lord's apartments. Hardly any extravagances of luxuries were spared in building the castle. Thomas Arundell renovated it into a Gothic style from the Renaissance one of Lord Lovel. The castle was besieged in 1643 doing great damage and was never repaired due to the extensive nature. A second castle was built later in 1756 to the Northwest now known as Wardour Castle.

The fate of Anne Boleyn led to a new marriage of significance leading to more than just anguish for all parties including the Howards and Arundells under the reign of Henry VIII. This marriage of great importance to the church was with Katherine Howard, the daughter of Edmund Howard. Katherine was also the sister-in-law of Thomas Arundell. At some time during the reign of Katherine, Queen of England, he became her Chancellor in administrative affairs due to being very wise in these matters. His performance at this position was notable and was held in high esteem by the Marquess of Dorset, who made him her Executor. Both Katherine and Thomas would not be given any dignities for their services as both would fall due to the reformations of Henry VIII. Katherine's services to the Crown were ended after formal apologies in 1542 and Thomas Arundell after formal letter of allegiance in 1552. During these reformations there are those who would fall on one side or the other such in the case of the War of the Roses.

The lands and manors obtained by Thomas Arundell or granted to by Henry VIII before his death are staggering in amounts documented and found in the late Wardour Castle. Many of them where retained by the grant of Henry VIII to Margaret Howard and many more were granted by Elizabeth I to Matthew Arundell, Margaret and Thomas Arundell's son, who also retook others. Wardour Castle remained in the hands of the Arundells and again they would reclaim their ancestral status that had been obtained throughout the centuries by valor and honor.

Foretold is the history of royal descent of the three lineages that can be traced back to Charlemagne, King of the Franks and Holy Roman Emperor, Merovigians, and the Trojans. The three lines of royal descent are separate but at the same time very much in union with each other as there are many marriages between them. The royal marriages between these three great Houses begin with Joan de Plantagenet de Cornwall, daughter of Richard de Cornwall de John "King of the Romans" in the marriage with John Howard, Norfolk Line. Margaret Mowbray, Dowager of Duke of Norfolk's marriage to Robert Howard was the next significant one between these houses and the second between Plantagenet lineage and Howard. John Arundell X married Elizabeth, the only major marriage between Plantagenets and Arundells. Thomas Howard, Duke of Norfolk, married Anne of York, Plantagenet, creating the third bond between the two Houses. Thomas Arundell married Margaret Howard and Katherine married Henry VIII Tudor in the turbulent time of the early sixteenth century. There must be special mention of the marriage between William Pincerna d' Albini, of the Ducal House of Normandy and his marriage to Adeliza of Louvania, Ducal House of Brabrant and Queen of England. Their bond was in the beginning of the golden era of England and was a glorious marriage with many children, honors, and above all practice and spreading of the Christian faith.

The coat of arms of the Arundells goes back to the ancient times of both France and England. From the Dukes of Normandy and Belgica they claim the lion and from Arundell they claim the six swallows from the Gaelic meaning taken from Soissons. The Arundells can also claim descendancy of Charlemagne by the same line as the Plantagenets starting from Herbert, Count of Vermandois. Their ancestry also goes back to the Ducal House of Normandy, Rollo and Robert I, upon which they drew their strength to accomplish what they had from the land wars in France to the Norman invasion of England to the battles in defending the Crown. The lineage of the Arundells also goes back to the Belgica area where the ancestors of Adeliza were from France and Germany. This line goes back three generations of Holy Roman Emperors including Charlemagne. The traits of the region of Soisson were passed onto to the landowners that first came to the region where the Arun River flowed. These men held the traits in the tradition of the swallow being very prompt to battle and expeditions. The Gaelic region of Soissons is the very region that Clovis won his first battle victory for the Franks as their King.

The Arundells were also a very Christian family who established churches, chapels, and monasteries throughout France and England. There are too many of them to name but the ones of great predominance have already been mentioned St. Sauvuer, St. Michaels, St. Albans, St. Columb, Affligem.

From the time Clovis the Great accepted Christianity the royal descendants of this divine journey have also accepted the faith intellectually, by baptism, and through spreading of its word to the populace. It would be over a sixteen hundred years of belief in Zeus (Jupiter) to guide and prosper the Trojan people after the fall of Troy to the time of Clovis. Another one thousand years would pass from his time of Christianity to the time of Sir Thomas Arundell, Lord of Wardour and Chancellor to the Queen of England Katherine Howard. Christianity had been fully accepted throughout the Continent of Europe and the Holy Roman Empire under Charles V and his successors the Habsburgs would insure its continuation and purpose given to the Temporal level of the divine will. This would require as throughout the time of the first Holy Roman Emperor Charles the Great men of valor and duty who drew upon their faith in God's will to aid in its increase beyond their own self-preservation. Two fronts had opened for the Holy Roman Empire, from the East by the Turks and to the West in the founding of the Americas. The former was in defense of the Empire and the latter would help spread the Empire's purpose. One or the other may have been in the minds of many but a descendant of the Arundells and Howards would aid in both. The blessing onto Judah by his father stating he would be the lion and many princes would come from him in many nations had come to pass by the precedence of Christianity.

VIII

ARUNDELL HOWARD

I presented myself at the front of the army where by reason of my plumes of feathers my armor bases and furniture all full of gold and silver a thing therefore altogether unusual I was presently marked of all men's eyes.

Baron Thomas Arundell of Wardour, "The Early Genealogical History of the House of Arundell" Yeatman 276

THE SPREADING OF CHRISTIANITY by both the Temporal and Spiritual levels of the divine will of God before the turn of the seventeenth century would have been considered favorable as it had been taken up by Clovis the Great, Charlemagne, Charles V, and then Rudolph II. A new struggle would begin between the Holy Roman Empire and a new adversary to the east and within the Christian faith. The Ottoman Empire and the Turks were on the rise in the east from the position they had taken from the Greeks in Constantinople. They were a formidable military and carried out constant attacks outside the realms of the Holy Roman Empire and Austria. Another struggle would come in the form of the split of the Christian Church in both Reformation and Counterreformation efforts. These two fronts would become the focus of both Charles V and Rudolph II of which the former would be victorious and the latter would be on negotiable terms. The Holy Roman Empire had not been dealt any defeats upon its creation in 800 under the reign of Charlemagne and this can be justified by its borders extending from the far eastern realms of Europe to England and the Mediterranean regions. This was accomplished by those who sought to spread its cause under considerable risk from Jerusalem to Constantinople to England. The precedence of the time would now become Duty and Faith. The duty by the Arundell Howards would be for their faith, Holy Roman Empire, country, and family. A period of four hundred years had passed since the time of William d' Albini and Adeliza of Louvania came to England to spread the Christian faith until Baron Thomas Arundell of Wardour took up the new precedence. The next four hundred years was for the duty of the four main priorities listed in hopes of continuation of prosperity.

Retaking of the Arundell manors, lands, and Wardour Castle by Matthew Arundell would be a significant victory, which would be consolidated by his son Baron Thomas Arundell of Wardour. The Arundells were seeking to become in better graces with the Crown and Elizabeth I after the struggle between them and Henry VIII and his reformation of the Church of England. The coming to terms and reconciliation would however take much longer than the generation of Baron Thomas Arundell of Wardour, and thus he sought other means of making a difference within the listed priorities.

It must be noted at this time concerning the surnames that will be used from this point on in this text. The marriage between Sir Thomas Arundell and Margaret Howard was a marriage between notable families of that time. Both Matthew Arundell and Baron Thomas Arundell are not shown to have taken the name of Howard as their own surname and at the same time they do not show to have pushed it away. It is not until Thomas Howard, who is the son of Baron Thomas Arundell of Wardour, that a name change is seen within the lineage. He is one of three brothers from the second marriage with Anne Thoroughgood who used the surname of Howard before or after they immigrated to America. The reason for the name change is not known, however, his sister Anne Arundell did not change her name. It most likely was for the prosperity of the surname of Howard and Arundell in America under the same family. It is for this reason that the name of Arundell Howard will be used only for the purposes of not losing sight of where the lineage had come from.

The Arundells to this time had not sought out things beyond the borders of England and were loyal only to their faith and the Crown of England. The reformation under Henry VIII and continuation of by Elizabeth I sent the next generation of Arundells into the outreached hand of the Catholic Faith and the Holy Roman Empire of Rudolph II of Austria under the Habsburgs. The honour of the family had been restored and now Baron Thomas Arundell of Wardour sought to strengthen the Catholic faith and gain leverage within the court of Elizabeth I. He did this through a duty to the Emperor and by his crusade to the outer realms of the Holy Roman Empire against the Ottoman Empire.

The reason for his departure on this crusade could be in light of the same reasons for Alexander the Great taking his valiant forces against the Persians or Richard the Lionheart going on crusade to Jerusalem. The reason for his crusade may have arisen from justice for the people, prosperity, defense of faith, and honour. The attack upon the Holy Roman Empire lands extending into Hungary by the Ottoman Empire was just such a cause to bring men of valor such as Baron Thomas Arundell of Wardour to the forefront of the battle. His valor in this just cause would gain him the same acclaim afterwards, as had the two previous mentioned great Kings.

Elizabeth I wrote a letter to Emperor Rudolph II of Austria, who she calls her August brother, cousin, and friend. In this letter she presents to him her cousin Baron Thomas Arundell of Wardour, enlightening the Emperor to the fact that he is considered her cousin and most importantly that he is of royal blood and his ancestors in England are derived from royal blood of Counts. This was most assuredly shown in the letter proceeding in this text by the following words:

> *Taking therefore into consideration your ancient and illustrious descent, which as I am assured by a letter from the most serene Princess and Lady Elizabeth I, Queen of England, France, and Ireland, our sister and cousin in the renowned Kingdom of England is derived from the Royal Blood. (Yeatman)*

This would be the accommodation Baron Thomas Arundell of Wardour would need to begin his crusade and duty to the Holy Roman Empire and the Emperor in a most virtuous, pious, and profound way.

The crusades of the tenth, eleventh, and twelfth centuries were conducted mainly in the region in and around Jerusalem with defense of its castles, lands and people as the main concern. These crusades were all successful in some degree, depending on the one discussed, and had many elite men as the leaders including Godfrey, Baldwin, Fulk V, Richard the Lionheart, Richard of Cornwall, and Edward I. The region of concern had now shifted in the sixteenth century to the region of the Austrian-Hungarian border with Constantinople at the center of the Ottoman Empire and Vienna at the Center of Austria and the Holy Roman Empire. This shift was due to the rise of the new Ottoman Empire under the Sultans and the Habsburg Emperors in Austria. A new battlefront began between men, armor, and faith that would cost many lives and create many men of valor and honour.

Baron Thomas Arundell of Wardour was known to have funded in 1591 the building of the Warspite, a Great class battleship, and at that same time left for the Spanish coast to travel to Austria/Hungary. Since Spain and Austria were both Catholic realms it would seem that one aided the other in letting Thomas arrive safely. Upon arrival to the battle area Baron Thomas Arundell of Wardour was unknown and not commanded by any military leader there. Although, more than likely since the preceding letter was sent to Emperor Rudolph II of Austria, his brother Matthias of Austria, who was in charge of military issues, knew of his arrival and his undertaking. It is said he immediately went to the front lines where he was fully armored and decked out in plumes of feathers and carried with him gold and silver furniture astonishing many within the army camp. The battle that would gain Baron Thomas Arundell of Wardour honors would now begin and the stage was set for many things afterwards. A great deal of interest was being attended to this battle and the parties of Elizabeth I, Emperor Rudolph II of Austria, Matthias of Austria, Spain, and the Ottoman Empire all had something to gain or lose from the battle undertaken in the region.

The Habsburgs were the reigning Emperors of the Holy Roman Empire at the time and had the most to lose or gain depending on the outcome of the war with the Turks. The Habsburgs were a dynasty that had been ongoing within the Austrian (southwestern Germany) region for over four centuries since the time of Rudolph of Habsburg was made king by the princes. The Habsburg's had established their predominance by historical and traditional weight of hereditary lands in this region, their family relation to the crown of the Holy Roman Empire, and the central power consolidation from Vienna. They absorbed power through the Imperial Crown and used it to establish policy for the Holy Roman Empire in the East which included Austria, Germany, Hungary, Croatia, Slovenia, Italy and many other regions. They held the Imperial Crown of the Holy Roman Empire up to the time of Baron Thomas Arundell of Wardour and after. The descendants of the Habsburgs are Albrecht II (1438-1452), Friedrich III (1452-1493), Maximilian (1493-1519), Charles V (1519-1556), Ferdinand I (1556-1564), Maximilian (1564-1576), Rudolph II (1576-1612), and Matthias I (1612-1619). They were subsequently holding the Crown until the year 1806 at the end of the reign of Francis II.

Emperor Rudolph II of Austria reigned during a period of great turmoil both within the Empire and outside from attacks at the farthest most boundaries in Hungary. He was born in Vienna on July 18, 1552 to Miximilian II, Holy Roman Emperor, King of Bohemia, King of Hungary, and mother Maria who was the daughter of Charles V, Holy Roman Emperor. The grandfather of both his father and mother was Philip I of Castile. Emperor Rudolph II was in constant struggle for the Crown with his brother Matthias of Austria, Governor of Austria, causing turbulence during the end of his reign in 1612 in the city of Prague. He reigned as King of Hungary in 1608 and King of Bohemia in 1611 which were later ceded to Matthias. Emperor Rudolph II was most tasked at the Reformation issue which caused religious strife within Austria and surrounding regions. He dealt with this issue first by counter-reformation and then later by issuing the royal charter *Majestat* (Letters of Majesty) in 1609 which guaranteed religious freedom for nobles and cities. His intellectual abilities outweighed his military abilities and for this reason he sought the unification of others to defeat the Turks in battle. These are the three reasons the Habsburgs were able to maintain their hold on the Imperial Crown: by creating a bond between their domains in the religious reformation and counter-reformation, creating a common defense system with their neighboring allies, and claiming hereditary lands which supplemented each other by economic means.

Two struggles by the Holy Roman Empire of reformation and the Ottoman Empire came to its first conclusion after the reign of Charles V. His devotion to the Catholic faith as the Habsburgs held to was transformed to these issues with sword and fire. Rudolph II brought a more sensible approach by compromise with ever increasing intolerance which would be called the counter-reformation. The religious issue was also brought under control for the need in unification against the Turks who were a threat to all in the region. Thus, counter-reformation and unification would be the sword of Rudolph II against the enemies of the Holy Roman Empire. The success in this can only be drawn by the defeat of the Turks and the continuation of the Habsburg Dynasty.

Emperor Rudolph II with his strategy in place and the Turks' refusal to honor the peace of Adrianople of 1568 made the decision to make the Turkish war his main concern lasting from 1593-1606 under the command of Matthias. The outcome of the war and the counter-reformation effort was to gain a standstill on one and move forward on the other. The Turkish War ended on a stalemate of counties given in negotiations and the counter-reformation ended in the Peace of Vienna in 1606.The underlying issues were that there was strife internal to the Empire, struggles between who was best to reign as Emperor, and an Ottoman Empire pressing in which brought about a great need for noblemen and soldiers outside the Empire to come and aid in its divine cause.

The Ottoman Empire was seeking to expand since the fourteenth century when it won a significant battle over the Byzantine Imperial army and the Greeks. The Sultans since the time of the Turcman chief named Osman were unrelenting in their ideological plan of conquering, consolidating, and rewarding. This plan made an empire by a constant movement of boundaries bringing in ever increasing population and then the spoils to the Ottoman army to continue the movement. This made for a continuous border movement which at the time of the sixteenth century had made contact with the Holy Roman Empire border with Hungary. The army of the Turks was known for its tactics of speed and mobility with less formidable troops up front and more disciplined ones in behind those. The Ottomans were also known for their nomadic impulse as they tended to be ever moving forward to the west.

A subsequent battle would begin and would continue in the region until the eighteenth century.

In 1595 the battle between the Holy Roman Empire and the Ottoman Empire had finally come to its high point. The Turks were using their position across the border into Hungary to launch attacks on Vienna for its silver. A tremendous amount of armour and weapons had been sent into the region to strengthen the military that were doing battle against the invading army. The battle Baron Thomas Arundell of Wardour fought would be one of many battles to come sending the Ottoman Empire into decline and it took place in a small city in northern Hungary about 50km northwest of the capital of Budapest .

Esztergom (Gran) lies on the right bank of the Danube river and was the capital of Hungary from the tenth to thirteenth century. The city was also the seat of the primate of the Roman Catholic Church. The region was inhabited by the Celts in 350 BC before Roman legions conquered the area next and then it was a border province of Pannonia during a migration period. The two major points of interest in the city are the palace where St. Stephen of Hungary was born on the Varhegy (Castle Hill) serving as the royal residence until 1241 and the basilica dedicated to St. Adalbert who baptized by St. Stephen. The church was the seat of the archbishop of Esztergom and was used in functions including crowning of kings. The castle and the basilica were devastated upon many attacks from 1543 to the battle of the Gran in 1595.

Devastation done to the infrastructure in Esztergom was extensive in the battle in which Baron Thomas Arundell of Wardour fought. The extent of the weapons used is not greatly known but for the period one could assume that armor, swords, explosives, and catapults could have been used. Baron Thomas Arundell of Wardour was with the troops that were under Count Karl Mansfeld and Baron Matyas Cseszneky. The three men of honour took the castle from the Turks on or before December 14, 1595 and Thomas brought down the standard, causing the Turkish troops to retreat. The castle which was being used as the staging ground for attacks and the headquarters of the front lines of the Ottoman Empire was now in the hands of the Holy Roman Empire. The significant names within the opposing military that were overtaken during these battles are unknown but it is most interesting to know that it is stated that on January 15, 1595 the sultan Murad III died of an ailment during his palace rest being entertained by music. This and other battles would end the westward movement of the Ottoman Empire and send it into decline, allowing the Emperor to begin resolving the internal issues of the Empire.

The valor done by Baron Thomas Arundell of Wardour would be recognized in formal attire upon his return to Prague from the battlefield. A letter was sent to the Emperor Rudolph II stating his extraordinary merit by the Marquis of Burgrave, the Arch Duke, and the Count of Selly. The return back to Prague was full of pomp and ceremony. The court and city were full of applause as the Emperor was present giving out rewards of sables, crystals, glasses, plates, and chains of gold. The Emperor then bestowed upon the soldier whose actions were most honorable in valor by patent an Earldom of the Empire as Count of the Holy Roman Empire. The decree written by His Imperial Majesty and presented on December 14, 1595 is as follows:

> **Rudolph II,** *by the favor of the Clemency always August, elected Emperor of the Roman Empire and Germany. King of Hungary, Bohemia, Dalmatia, Croatia, Slavonia, Ect. Arch Duke of Austria, Duke of Burgundy, Brabant, Etiria, Carinthia, Carniola, Ect. Marquise of Moravia, Ect. Duke of Lucenburg, and of Higher and Lower Silesia, Wertemberg, Ect. Prince of Suavia, Count of Habsburg, Tyrol, Kyburg, and Goritia; Landgrave of Alsatia; Marquis of Burgovia of the Sacred Roman Empire, and of Higher and Lower Lusatia, Ect. Lord of the Marquisate of Sclavonia, Ect. To our illustrious and sincerely beloved* **Thomas Arundell,** *Count of the Sacred Roman Empire, our Imperial Favour, and every thing that is good. Whereas we, according to our innate benign disposition and the Clemency and Example of the great and immortal God, who showers down in a copious manner the abundance of his heavenly Liberality on Mankind (after that, by his divine Majesty, we were called and raised up to this human Majesty, and the Right of the Imperial Dignity), have nothing more at Heart (in order that the Renown of our Empire may be rendered more conspicuous and illustrous) than that our Munificence may be fully extended and exercised towards all those whose bravery and fidelity deserve it: yet we think it highly necessary that a diligent and singular regard be had that a proper distinction be observed in conferring rewards, honours and dignities on men's deserts; namely, that one may be distinguished from another, by some higher degrees of honour; that those who are more nobly descended, who, by their brave and illustrious actions, and their regard of virtue; and by strenuously exerting themselves for the good of their country, and their Princes, greatly add to those virtues derived from their ancestors, should be advanced to higher degrees of honour and dignity; for thus a due observance of justice and equity is maintained and the minds of others by their illustrious examples are excited to a becoming emulation of virtue and glory. Taking therefore into consideration your ancient and illustrious descent, which (as I am assured by a letter from the most*

serene Princess and Lady Elizabeth, Queen of England, France, and Ireland, our sister and cousin) in the renowned Kingdom of England is derived from the Royal Blood; and those eminent virtues likewise by which you render the splendor of your family more illustrious both at home and abroad; whereas your first care was to furnish your mind with the knowledge of all good and useful literature; you have traveled foreign countries, have seen many different cities, and their customs, by which you have acquired much advantage; whereas finally you have come at so great a distance into Hungary at your own expense (excited thereto by a singular and unusual zeal to bear arms under us in this sacred war, which w wage against the Turk the common enemy of the Christian name; and have behaved yourself with such undaunted bravery, both in the open field, and in besieging cities and camps, as to be held in general admiration and we have received more ample testimonies in your favour from the most Serene Prince Arch Duke Matthias, our dear brother, and from the commanding officers of our army; this eminent instance of your bravery, amongst others being observed, that in the besieging of the lower town near Gvan, you, with you own hand, took the banner from the tower, and, during the engagement placed your self in the front of the army; which eminent services we would by no means, pass by without bestowing upon you and your legitimate posterity, some distinguishing mark of our favour. Out of our own motion therefore, from our certain knowledge, with a well deliberated mind and having taken proper counsel thereon, We by our full Imperial Authority and Power, have created, made, and nominated you, the aforesaid **Thomas Arundell** *(who before this time derive from your ancestors in England the consanguinity of Counts) and all and every of your children, heirs, and legitimate descendants of both sexes, already born, or that ever hereafter shall be true Counts and Countesses of the sacred Roman Empire: and we have granted and ennobled you with the Title, Honour and Dignity of the Empire, as by the tenor of these presents, we do create, make, nominate, grant, and ennoble. Willing, and firmly, and expressly decreeing by this our Imperial Patent, which will be always in force, that you the aforesaid* **Thomas Arundell** *with all, and every of your children and legitimate posterity, both male and female for ever do have, possess and assume for ever, the Title, Stile and Dignity of Counts of the Empire: and that you be honoured called and stiled by the Title, both in writing, and speaking in things spiritual and temporal ecclesiastical and prophane. And finally that you freely, and without any impediment, use, enjoy, obtain and partake of all, and every of* *the honours, ornaments, dignities, grants, liberties, priviledges, rights, ancient customs, preheminences and prerogatives, which our other Counts of the Sacred Roman Empire enjoy, use, and partake of law or custom not making any impediment, or requiring any thing contrary to these; and if there were any such laws or customs, particular and express, mention ought to be made in these presents: all and every of which impediments, we do by our Imperial Authority knowingly make void, and will and declare to be sufficiently void by these presents (so that the rights and priviledges of the most Serene Princess Elizabeth, Queen of England, France, and Ireland, our most dear Sister and Cousin remain safe and secure). Let no one therefore of whatever Degree, State, Order, Condition, or Dignity, or whatever high rank or station he may be of, revoke, or by any rash attempt contradict this our confirmation, ratification, approbation, corroboration, execution, will favour and decree: whosoever shall do this, let him know by these presents, that he ipso facto, incurs our very severe displeasure, and that of the Sacred Roman Empire; and that he shall likewise be fined in the penalty of one hundred marks of pure gold; half of which we decree to be paid into our Imperial Treasury, and the other to be paid and applied for the use of the injured (without the least hopes of pardon or remission). In testimony of these Letters we have subscribed our hand and fixed our Imperial Seal: Given at our Royal Palace at Prague, the 14 Day of December in the Year of our Lord 1595, in the 21 Year of our Reign of the Empire; of Hungary the 24; of Bohemia the 21. (Yeatman)*

A period of two years had passed since Baron Thomas Arundell of Wardour arrived in Prague prepared for battle against the invading Turks upon the Holy Roman Empire. He was now bestowed with great honors for his services by the Emperor Rudolph II and would return to England with a different kind of welcome. His return to England would be by way of a damaged Warspite during the Spanish Armada captain by Sir Walter Raleigh. The Crown of England had succeeded from Elizabeth I (Tudor), James I (James VI of Scotland, Stuart), and James II (Stuart) and all had different views of the accomplishment and valor shown by Thomas for the Holy Roman Empire. The recognition of the new Title bestowed on Thomas by the Crown was a slow process due to the state of affairs regarding the reformation, the Habsburgs, and Spain.

Recognition by Elizabeth I would not be forthcoming as the Queen of England believed subjects of the Crown should pay attention to the issues of England and not seek out honors from foreign Crowns. James I would be more flexible in this matter and made Thomas Arundell of Wardour a Baron for his accomplishment overseas but did not go as far as to recognize his Count Title. Finally, on March, 20, 1686 James II wrote a document of recognition to a large number of nobles within the Court and to the family members of Baron Thomas Arundell of Wardour. The Holy Roman Empire by the act of James II had extended its dominions into England and America based on the immigration of Baron Thomas Arundell of Wardour sons and daughter.

During the period between 1597-1630 Baron Thomas Arundell of Wardour was allowed to sail the high seas after a falling out with Elizabeth I. He used this time to travel with Sir Walter Raleigh on the Warspite to areas of America and South America in search of the El Dorado, which they finally sought out in an area of Venezuela. After these travels he used the Warspite he inherited after the death of Somerset and Raleigh to sail to America in 1630 to buy land granted by Sir Robert Cecil. The Warspite afterwards would be used for only harbor duty. This would be the last journey of Baron Thomas Arundell of Wardour who died in 1639.

The issue of recognition in the beginning of the seventeenth century was not foremost in Baron Thomas Arundell of Wardour's priorities. He now sought out counsel and men of great measure in plans to aid his family in immigration to the new lands of America. The populace on the other side of the reformation movement and who sought to avoid the Thirty Years War along with the civil strife in England looked to new frontiers to practice the freedom of religion and the prosperity that could be obtained. The reformation in England brought about expulsions of bishops, priests, and the followers from the kingdom and set zealous leaders from the other side against the Crown of England. The European reformation was significantly worse as the Holy Roman Empire and its allies fought against the alliance for reformation. The Thirty Years War took a great toll especially in Germany where the population dropped by an estimated 8,000,000 between 1618 and 1648. The Treaty of Westphalia was meant to resolve the religious, political, and constitutional issue between the warring parties. The breakdowns from civilians up to the Crown in both England and Europe was enough for Thomas and others to seek out men with influence and skill such as Robert Cecil, Captain George Weymouth, George Calvert and his son Cecilius Calvert for voyages across the Atlantic to set up colonies in America.

A voyage to New England in 1603 had brought back a good report from Captain Martin Pring, which consequently increased the interest of Baron Thomas Arundell of Wardour and the Earl of Southhampton. In 1605 they sent out their own Captain George Weymouth to Kennebec on a scouting mission, which also brought back encouraging reports. The other two main events of this time were Queen Elizabeth I's death in 1603 and the peace given by Spain in 1605 making voyages to America more secure even though neither England or Spain ceded territorial claims. Plans were now quickly drawn up based on good reports to attempt colonization through joint stock companies. The two companies formed were the Plymouth Company, whose chief patron was Robert Cecil the secretary of state, and the London Company whose chief patron was John Popham the chief justice. Land was given out in tracts of one hundred yard miles fronting the sea and one hundred miles extending into shore. The London Company was given the First Colony and the Plymouth Company given the Second Colony. These colonies were to set up councils of which laws, ordinances, and instructions were to be given by James I, the reigning King England.

The attempts to settle in America prior to the plans of Baron Thomas Arundell of Wardour and George Calvert, the first Lord Baltimore, were that of the Jamestown settlement of 1607 and that of the Virginia Company and the Mayflower in 1620 which was set off course from Virginia to New England. It was now George Calvert's attempt of colonizing America that would found Maryland for the religious relief of his settlers. George Calvert was from Yorkshire and was the private secretary of Robert Cecil, who was knighted in 1617. The Land that was sought out by him was along the Potomac River bordering Virginia. He obtained a patent from the Crown Mariana in honor of King Charles' wife Henrietta Maria. It was later changed from Terra Mariae to Maryland. In 1632 George Calvert died and passed the charter onto his son Cecil Calvert who had studied at Trinity College, Oxford University. He married Anne Arundell, the daughter of Baron Thomas Arundell of Wardour who had ties to his father. In 1633 the second Lord Baltimore set sail for America with ships *Ark* captained by Richard Lowe and the *Dove* captained by Richard Orchard. The ships took a course from England to the Canary Islands then to the Barbados and next to Point Comfort up the Chesapeake Bay to St. Clement's Island.

A passenger list that traveled on the *Ark* and *Dove* do not show Anne Arundell or the assumed passengers of her three brothers, documented in genealogy by Yeatman, of Thomas, Frederick, and Matthew. However, Thomas is noted to have transported himself to America in 1647 and probably on the ship inherited from his father by funds the Warspite. Traveling at the time was risky due to continental tensions and at the same time uprisings were beginning within the American Colonies and a show of force may have been a necessity. In light of this matter Lord Calvert was recorded on the ship and it would be a fair assumption that his wife was traveling with him. Royalty leaving their own country at the time was seen as a significant matter especially to the Crown and court. In 1634 the county of St. Mary's was laid out by Leonard Calvert and succeeding counties of Kent (1642), Charles, and Anne Arudelin (1650) would follow. Thomas Arundell Howard, the son of Baron Thomas Arundell of Wardour, was granted on December 20, 1653. "Howard's Mount" in the Newton Hundred in St. Mary's County, Maryland (known as St. Clement's Island) is shown on Mernards' Map. This purchase may have been part of an earlier one made by Baron Thomas Arundell of Wardour in his voyage to America in 1630.

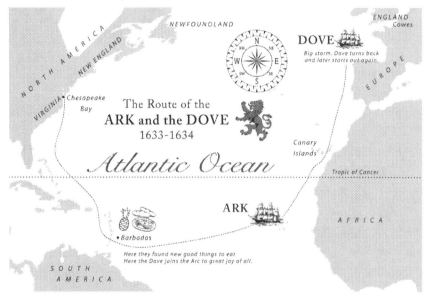

It was nearly six centuries earlier when the Arundell ancestor William d' Albini accompanied William Duke of Normandy onto the shores of England in battle with the Anglo-Saxons in 1066. The only struggle for the immigrants of America would be in a small degree native Indians. The two tribes that had settled in the Maryland region were the Algonquin Indians and the Yaocomaco Indians who were both kind in nature and willing to help the colonists in acquiring food and clearing land for planting. Over time the native Indians moved away due to differences and tensions with the colonists.

Lord Baltimore set the colony up in a manorial system that included landlords and tenants The hierarchical system put the sons of prominent Roman Catholic families as heads of manors with settlers as tenant farmers. These manors were erected on land grants and entitled the owner to name it by their own personal wishes. Thomas Arundell Howard had named his manor "Howard's Mount" and his son William "Captain" Arundell Howard would later own "Pomfret Field" and "Twitnam" all within St. Clement's Island. Pomfret Field was most likely named after the Earl and Countess of

Pomfret, England. Dowager Countess Henrietta Louisa was the owner of many statues and marbles relating to the Arundell marbles mentioned earlier from the collection of Thomas Howard, Earl of Arundell. She is most known for dedicating the marbles to Oxford University in 1755.

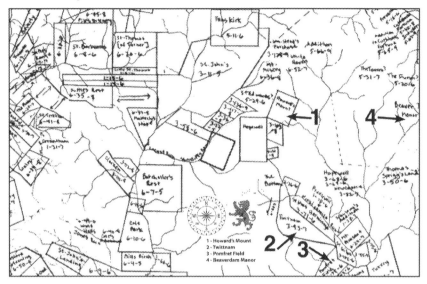

The Arundell Howards came from Wiltshire, England where the family held Wardour Castle and as stated Thomas Arundell Howard came with his family who settled in the Maryland and Virginia areas. The families they came to marry from 1647 to 1792 would be from Kent (Wakefield's), York (Spink's), Lincolnshire (Smith's), and Inverness, Scotland (Logsdon's). Most of these families had settled in the area of Charles County, Maryland before their marriages within the Arundell Howard family. The Arundell Howards did continue the family tradition of military duty and support in some degree to the Crown in England. This is evident in the son and grandson of Thomas Arundell Howard by William Howard Sr. (1662 – 1730), who was called and known to be Captain, and William Howard, Jr. (1696 – 1753), who in his will mentions two military officers in Captain George Clark and Captain Justian Jordan, both from St. Mary's County, Maryland. In what capacity the officers of this colonial time performed duties is hard to say but more than likely it was to keep order in what soon would become disorder on many fronts. Due to religious issues that erupted in 1689 the government of the colony was taken control by a royal governor under William and Mary in 1691 lasting twenty four years. The beginning of the British Empire foothold in America was beginning to take shape and would be contested by France in battles that would last from 1754 – 1771 called the Seven Year War.

Timeline England and Maryland: Arundell Howard

America	England		Europe	

Events Leading to Immigration

America	England		Europe	
	1591	Baron Thomas Arundell of Wardour funds Warspite and leaves for Austria/ Hungary		
			Aug. 1595	Spanish Armada
			Dec. 1595	Count of HRE Decree
	1595	Transported back to England on Warspite		
			1597	Thomas allowed to sail the seas with Sir Walter Raleigh El Dorado on Warspite
	1600	Birth of Frederick Arundell Howard		
	1603	Death of Elizabeth I		
	1605	Captain Weymouth sails to America		
	1606	Birth of Thomas Arundell Howard		
1607 Jamestown Settlement				

1609	Birth of Matthew Arundell Howard		
		1612	Death Rudolph II
	1615 Birth of Anne Arundell		

Events Leading to Monarchy

1620 Mayflower sails to America

1630 Baron Thomas sails to America on Warspite to buy land grant

1633 Landing of Arch December

1634 Landing of Dove January

1634 Manorial Landowner set up by Lord Baltimore

1634 Lord Baltimore assemblies at St. Mary

Events leading to British Control

1639 Death of Baron Thomas Arundell of Wardour

1641 English Civil War

1645 Religious Uprising

1647 Thomas Arundell Howard transports to America on Warspite

	1649	Death of Anne Arundell
1659	Death of Matthew Arundell Howard	
	1661	Royal Army Started
	1666	Second Warspite commissioned used for colonial travel
	1686	James II Recognition of Count
1687	Death of Thomas Arundell Howard	
1691	Resign by Lord Baltimore	
1754	Seven Years War	
1754	Brig. Gen. Clement Howard	
1758	Third Warspite (*Arundell*) commissioned	
1775	Revolutionary War	
1776	Clement Howard enlist	

The Arundell Howard family that came to America were descendants of Baron Thomas Arundell of Wardour, a soldier of fortune in Europe for the Holy Roman Emperor Rudolph II, and the Arundells of Lanherne, England. The descendants would carry on the illustrious tradition of military honors as Clement Howard, Sr. (1726 –1772) by tradition, as narrated by Rev. H. B. Schulte of St. Mark's Catholic Church and ordained at St. Mary's Seminary in Baltimore, also a member of the Kentucky State Historical Society, had become a Brigadier General in the British Army, four ranks higher than his grandfather William Howard, Sr. during the time of the Seven Years War. Clement, also having found favor from his father for doing his will, was thus granted by William Howard, Jr. lands in St. Mary's County, Maryland after his death. The Arundell Howard family would now take up the their duty for the British Empire, the Crown, the Colonial States, and later the Continental Army from 1754 – 1783 until the end of the Revolutionary War. The Arundell Howards to some degree were set into a condition of binding together three loyalties they may have been compelled to be of service and duty: to the British Empire, the Colonial families, and the Holy Roman Empire by their Catholic Faith. A discovery of each of these is in order to show how they journeyed through this time period and maintained both duty and faith.

The Seven Years war, also known as the French and Indian War, lasted from 1754 – 1763 and was a struggle worldwide as the British Empire set out to distinguish with the aid of the colonists the French occupation in the Americas as well as involvement in tensions on the European Continent between Austria, Prussia, Russia, and France. In 1753 an emissary under Major George Washington was sent into the Ohio Country with the hopes of ending the building of forts by the French that King George II was greatly disapproving. The twenty year old Major in the British Army accepted the task but it would end in a bloody fight bringing two Empires at odds over the lands from Canada to the interior of the Continent of Ohio and then outward to the Colonial coast. The fourteen colonies from Novia Scotia to Georgia would now come under battle with the French and their allies the Indians.

On the European front the three nations Britain, Austria, and Russia were becoming allied to stop the military advance of France and Prussia from taking control of Hanover, which England had ties, and Silesia, which Austria had ties. Austria under the reign of Empress Maria Theresa sought to counter any offensive by Frederick of Prussia and in so doing made temporary alliances with France to keep the peace. In 1757 Prussia would end the peace by invading Austria only to lose large numbers of infantry and causing tensions to once again rise on the European Continent. These alliances and friction within the European Continent would continue until 1803 and the end of the Napoleonic Wars.

The condition of the Seven Years War in America for the British position in 1756 was unstable. The causes were threefold in that the changing of command created non-continuity, the French had used the Indian alliance effectively, and the cost of the war to build forts, roads and outposts had become burdening to the British Empire. Other problems arose in regards to the lack of wagons and teams to pull materials and men across the wilderness terrain and the roads built for General Braddock's military campaigns. The continuous setbacks and the defeat at Monongahela left the British officers with nobody to blame but the colonists for their lack of support and in some aspect unprofessional character in battle situations. In return the colonists blamed the professional army and felt they sought only their own glory in battle and not the well being of the colonists. Colonists sought to be patriots in a war that only the British Empire could be victorious in. To eliminate all these issues the British commanders came to the conclusion to create a Continental Army under the command of George Washington and to change the colonists' purpose from a battle engaging force to one of revenue by way of taxation. The former would give substance to revolution and the latter would give reason for action.

The British Army and Navy were reinstated by Charles II in 1661 for royal security and to remove any contention with the Crown. The British officer was one who was compelled to do his duty because it was his livelihood and victory for England would bring financial gains for them. Therefore, only one allegiance to the monarchy was given from that time to the Seven Years War.

The British officer was to overlook the building of roads, forts, and outposts along with putting down domestic disputes and engaging the French and Indians when necessary. The three main roads built were the Forbes Road, Crown Point Road and Braddock Road extending from Carlisle, Pennsylvania and Alexandria, Maryland up to Pittsburgh where the three rivers of the Ohio, Allegheny, and Monongahela met. Forts that stood between 1754 – 1763 were Ft. Federick, Ft. Loudon, Ft. Bedford, Ft. Prince George, Ft. Allen, Ft. Cumberland and many others by both the French and British armies. Naval forces were given the task of blockading the French fleet from trade on the continent and if necessary engaging them in battle. The usual battle tactics were to sail parallel to the enemy in rows of ships with the wind behind their sails and to slowly pass by while tearing into the French ships with their battle guns blazing. This was done mostly to damage the ship beyond use and not to sink them. During the 1750s the *Arundell* (third Warspite built renamed) was commissioned for naval service with its seventy four cannons a formidable battleship used in the same sailing tactic as stated.

For the purpose of this book four distinct men of significance in both the Seven Years War, Revolutionary War, and afterward will be discussed: Clement Howard (Sr. and Jr.), George Washington, and Daniel Boone. Each made a difference in some degree to the British effort in the French and Indian War, and then looked for a better and higher cause of liberty in the Revolutionary Army and after the end of both struggles looked to the western frontier in search of prosperity.

George Washington was from Virginia and grew up there before seeking out a military career. In 1752 he was a Major in the British Army under General Braddock. During his service he fought in military campaigns in the three river area in the Ohio country having differing results. He became the Commander of the Continental Army in 1754 with duties in Virginia to train the colonials for battle. In this venture he became a quite efficient leader who expected discipline within his ranks. These forces he commanded during the Seven Years War were to aid the British regulars in carrying out their defined missions. After the war he would use his tested and well trained army to defeat the same ones he had been aiding.

Daniel Boone was from Rowan County, North Carolina and was a formidable soldier as well as backwoodsmen and hunter. He served under many British officers during the Seven Years War including Major General Dobb's North Carolina militia during General Braddock's ill fated attempt for victory at Fort Duquesne, General John Forbe's Virginia troops, and Major Hugh Waddell's Cherokee campaigns. Boone became an excellent soldier, scout, explorer, and hunter during his campaigns and travels up to the end of the war in 1763. He would use these skills to push further outward into Florida, Tennessee, Kentucky and Missouri.

Clement Howard, Sr. was from St. Mary County , Maryland where he owned land and did services in the British Army as Brigadier General. He was the great-grandson of Thomas Arundell Howard, who was son of the recognized Count Thomas Arundell of Wardour by James II. This royal status and being in the royal army put him in a rare position as he was a Royalist who sought out a fresh start in new lands while attempting to gain favor from the Crown. The Governor of Maryland and the Assembly had decided to sit out the Seven Years War and oppose the commander and chief's instructions. The farthest the legislature of the state of Maryland would allow colonial troops to move was Ft. Frederick. British officers such as Captain John Dagworthy in Maryland had a royal commission and they performed their duty to the Crown by handing down orders to the lower ranks like Colonel George Washington of Virginia who had only a provincial commission. Thus using one's rank and royal commission to set out what needed to be done to the regular army and playing the part of British patrol from Maryland to Ft. Frederick as well as being the rear to General Braddock's westward military efforts and naval support on the coast was the duty held by a Maryland Royal Officer of Britain. The Maryland coast was under continual attack due to trade prospects by the French needed to be addressed and any patrol outside of a fort in the back country was subject to enemy raids. Maryland eventually would become a prototype to the colonies after the Seven Year War in respect to its governing, assemblies, trade, and standing up to the British commanders' instructions resulting in the Revolutionary War.

In 1760 the war was drawing to a close and it finally came to a realization that the professional army and colonial army could work together in defeating the French and Indian alliance. The British would now seek the rewards from this victory by allying with the Indians, gaining revenue from the colonists by taxation, and controlling settlements outside the already established colonies. This grand plan would be matched by the colonists' own ideas for the future and the French who were resentful in defeat and ready to make retribution.

Tensions would rise steadily after 1760 between Britain's army and the colonial assemblies and its provincial soldiers. The main factors had come to a boiling point and they were in regards to who had become the benefactor in the war against the French and Indians, the Mutiny Act enacted, the Quartering Act enacted, and the Stamp Act. These orders which came down by Britain were to aid in its goals for the Empire in America while the colonists saw them as acts of submission, degrading to their lifestyles, and putting the burden onto them for finances. This led to the main views of the colonists of equality, rights, and liberty. Finally in 1768 a clash between the British army and a civil mob in Boston left many dead in the streets, setting the stage for conflict between the British Empire and the Continental Colonies.

George Washington on July 3, 1775 would become commander of the Continental Army and the New England regiments underneath him would be the beginning of the turning point from revolt to revolution in which he as a seasoned soldier and commander during the Seven Years War was most suited for the task as the Continental Congress supported him in this position. His defeats as a British officer and tenure as commander over the Virginia regiments helped strengthen his contention for victory over the British regulars.

On July 4 the Continental Congress approved the Declaration of Independence after one year of initial warfare. The ideals of equality, rights, and liberty were now worth a great struggle that would occur for the colonists and the Continental Army. There is little doubt that as a British officer Clement Howard, Sr. could see what type of situation this had become before his death in 1772. His son Clement Howard, Jr. was now twenty six years of age and to no doubt learned from his father about military matters and assumedly came to the same conclusion both personally and military wise what might be the outcome of this war. On July 25, 1776 he enlisted in the revolutionary army in Maryland by Ensign Nathan Williams. He had evidently come to a determination that the Revolutionary War would be worth fighting for both prosperity in the future and militarily on the battlefield that would last until 1783. As all the ancestors before had made their decisions on what is righteous and what is unjustified or for glory's sake, so had the Arundell Howards in America sought out righteousness in hopes that God would prevail. Their faith gave them the strength to serve both family and country properly even back to the times of St. Sauvuer.

In 1774 a new a conflict had begun called the Indian War, which was a result of Cherokee attacks in the Ohio and Kentucky regions. This was also called Lord Dunmore's War, for he is the one Governor who brought together an assembly to resolve the issue of Indian attacks. During the war Daniel Boone was to act as both a scout and military man to locate the enemy and find routes into the region. Upon doing so he would lose his son to the Indians which would not be the only family loss he would encounter during his days in Kentucky. Despite attacks from the Indians, mainly the Shawnee, a fort was established on the Kentucky River in 1775 and it was called Boonesborough. Boone had many difficulties in defending the new fort for he was both shot in the ankle and taken prisoner for a time period by the Shawnee in 1778. He would also join George Rogers Clark from 1780 – 1783 in fighting the Shawnee in the Ohio country. His services to the colonies was not in fighting in the Revolutionary War effort but in seeking to resolve attacks against them by the Indians in Virginia and westward in order for future settlements to occur, which could be considered the secondary front in the Revolutionary War.

The Revolutionary War would come to a close and liberty was won by the efforts of men of valor whose sole duty was to be victorious on the side of righteousness and religious freedom. Clement Howard, Jr. now sought the rewards of accomplishments during twenty nine years of struggle between his duty and his father's. He would now take his family to the prosperous lands of Kentucky in 1791 where he settled in Madison County and built a Plantation to the west of the Kentucky River and Boonesborough. Clement was the first of many Catholic families to come to Kentucky, others include Durbin, Wagers, and Logsdon. In the area they settled just west of Boonesborough they named the creeks running off the Kentucky River "Howard's Upper Creek" and "Howard's Lower Creek". The order of Our Lady of Trappe founded a monastery on Pottinger Creek in 1785 and called it St. Rose. A bishop of the See, Reverend Benedict Joseph Flaget, was given episcopal jurisdiction early in June 1811. The Howard and the Boone families would now come in first contact with each other as Daniel is reported to have hunted on the Kentucky River as late as 1793. Two military men with ancestors that go back to England with one of the Catholic Faith, the other of Quaker had come to the same place with the same ideals in mind for their faith, family, and country. The state of Kentucky was accepted by petition from President George Washington as the fifteenth state on June 1, 1792 continuing the westward movement.

On the European Continent a new revolution was brewing in France and the bloodshed would not end until both King and Queen had met their death. Marie Antoinette had become entangled in a web of conflict within the political assembly and financial issues. The Queen of France was of the Habsburg Royalty daughter of Francis I, Holy Roman Emperor, and Empress Maria Theresa of Austria who still maintained a dynasty in Austria at the time. She married King Louis XVI of France (1774) at the young age of fourteen when he was the Dauphin of France. General Napoleon Bonaparte rose from this revolution and would now seek to unify Europe in what some would consider tyranny rather than a righteous Emperor. The Holy Roman Empire would now struggle against an Emperor with a different diet other than Christianity as a precedence for the people.

A new order began under Francis II, Holy Roman Emperor (1792 – 1806), Emperor of Austria (1804 –1835), the grandson of Empress Maria Theresa and Emperor Francis I. Under his reign Austria and the Holy Roman Empire battled with France and Napoleon several times but in the end an alliance of nations to aid Francis II against the tyranny of Napoleon would become victorious in 1813. Before this conclusion to hostilities Napoleon in 1806 established a Confederation of the Rhine and Francis II renounced his Imperial Title as Holy Roman Emperor. The suspension of the Empire by Emperor Francis II occurred after the fall of Napoleon and the abdication and renunciation of the Imperial Title and Crown for himself. From this time on the Imperial Title and Crown would lay dormant. The Holy Roman Empire would go into a dormant phase seeking a less predominant role in civil and political affairs than previously. The ideas that had been built upon since Charlemagne was crowned Emperor in 801 AD up to the last Emperor in 1806 are proposed by St. Augustine in the "City of God" as he states the following in regards to this condition.

> *"But in the family of the just man who lives by faith and is as yet a pilgrim journeying on to the celestial city, even those who rule serve those whom they seem to command; for they rule not from a love of power, but from a sense of the duty they owe to others- not because they are proud of authority, but because they love mercy."*

Charlemagne was a much merciful King of the Franks and Holy Roman

Emperor during the first reign of the Temporal alongside the Spiritual of the Pope while giving alms to all in his Empire and beyond its borders.

A duty has been done by the Arundell Howards since the time of Baron Thomas Arundell of Wardour went to Austria under Matthias to turn the tide of battle against the Muslim invading army. They have done their duty for the Holy Roman Empire, Christianity, Austria, England, Colonial America, family, friends, and God. The faith of Baron Thomas Arundell of Wardour brought him the strength to do the will of God as did Thomas Arundell Howard who came to America with his faith to guide him through the difficulties to be encountered along the way. Both Clement Howard, Sr. and Clement Howard, Jr. would rely on their faith to make the right decision for their country and family and to once again bring prosperity and Christianity to new lands.

The Arundell Howards continued to seek out new horizons like their ancestors the St. Sauvuers of Normandy. Duty and faith was still the precedence which they sought to bring forth prosperity for all. Their family and friends would become of major importance during these times of new horizons. Clement Howard, Jr. had thirteen children, considered remarkable during these times of the Revolutionary War and hardships. Two that will be mentioned are Phillip Howard and Sabrena Howard. A marriage between Phillip and Lenorah Wyatt would bring them even closer to the Boone family in Kentucky. The Wyatts were from Rowan County, North Carolina as was the Boone family. They came to Madison, Kentucky in 1803, nearly the same time as the Arundell Howards. The marriage between Sabrena and Joseph Ambrose Durbin would bring two other families together. Sabrena's sister Mary Ann had married him previously but then passed away. All these families, Arundell Howard, Boone, Durbin, Wyatt, and Webb would end up in the gateway to the west, Missouri, and have marriages between them.

In 1799 Daniel Boone and his kin Hays, Bryan, and Callaway had moved to the state of Missouri in what is now St. Charles County. Deaths in the Boone family during the time were Susannah (Boone) Hays in 1800 and Rebecca (Boone) Goe in 1805. James Monroe had granted Daniel Boone 1,000 acres of land in Missouri and finally in 1820 he passed away and was interred next to Rebecca in Tuque Creek. This would not be the end of the Boone descendants as the Goe family still lived in Kentucky for some time after the death of Daniel Boone.

The move to the west was in the minds of the Arundell Howards and Durbin family too as they settled in Dekalb County, Missouri sometime after 1850. The settlement of the Boone family was approximately in St. Louis, while Phillip Howard and the Durbins settled near Kansas City, Missouri on the border of Kansas and Nebraska. This at the time was the outermost territory of the plains in the west, having been previously scouted out by George Rogers Clark. During this time period in Missouri, Mary Francis Howard, the daughter of Phillip, married Benjamin Turner Goe. Benjamin was the son of Nathan B. Goe and grandson of Rebecca (Boone) Goe, a daughter of Daniel and Rebecca Boone. Sabrena would also travel with her brother Phillip to Missouri where she too would pass away. The ancestors to the Durbins can be traced to the state of Oregon, for when researching these times it had come to an acquaintance with a Durbin who knew of Sabrena, Phillip, and Clement Howard, Jr. from their own family history.

There would now be a new duty for the Arundell Howards to accept by the grandson of Phillip, Jordan Howard II. His duty would come at the age of twenty-four and it would be solely voluntary in the Spanish American War (1899) in the tradition of the Arundell Howard family. This duty would be a long hard one to Cuba and the Spanish held coasts in what would be called Teddy Roosevelt's "Rough Riders". The history of the making of the "Rough Riders" and their travels to the Spanish held lands for the battles they would engage in reads like the special forces gathering for a mission of success or total failure.

The first step taken up was to organize the troops to be taken and to have them ready to sail against either the Cuban or the Spanish coasts. The sign up places for the regiments who were to be non-voluntary in nature were appointed in New Mexico, Arizona, Oklahoma, and Indian Territory. The task of raising the regiment was not more than a day or two after it was announced when it literally was deluged with applications from every quarter of the Union. From the men who did apply an elite group were selected who showed the ability of arming, equipping, mounting, and discipline. Hundreds of regiments were being called for arms by the National Government and each regiment had its own needs to fulfill for the journey. Other selected men within the State troops were already organized as National Guard units trained and fit for battle. The volunteers, however, had not seen anything like the fighting expected of them. The only organized bodies to be immediately accepted were those from the four Territories mentioned. However, because the number of men originally allotted of 780 was speedily raised to 1,000 a chance to accept quite a number of eager volunteers who did not come from the Territories was opened. These volunteers who were expected to possess precisely the same temper that distinguished the southwestern recruits and those who materially benefited the regiments, were readily taken into consideration.

Regiments entered upon their duties as troopers in the spirit they held to the end. They were men that could show that no work could be too hard, too disagreeable, or too dangerous for them to perform and neither asking nor receiving any reward in the way of promotion or consideration. All the men selected into the "Rough Riders" sought more than hard work, rough fare, and the possibility of death. These men of both non-volunteer and volunteers turned out to be such good soldiers, largely due to the fact that they were men that thoroughly counted the cost before entering and who went into the regiment because they believed that this offered their best chance for seeing hard and dangerous service. Characteristics that could be expected from the men selected were the ability to handle wild and savage horses, following the chase with the rifle both for sport and as a means of livelihood, hardened to life in the open, and to handle themselves under adverse circumstances. Some of them came from the small frontier towns seeking new and more stirring adventures beyond the sea. These were the men that made up the regiments of the "Rough Riders". From all social positions, each man possessed in common the traits of hardship and a thirst for adventure.

The leaders of the regiments' first task was to make them ready for action in the shortest possible time. Fighting was very much expected as soon as land was met and some regiments might be the first expedition that left the United States. Allyn Capron was one of the leaders of the regiments and he required instant obedience and tolerated not the slightest evasion of duty. He possessed a mastery of his art and his performance of his own duty was so rigid that he won at once not merely the soldiers' admiration, but that soldierly affection so readily given by the men in the ranks to the superior who cares for his men and leads them fearlessly in battle.

Regiments were transported by rail from San Antonio to Tampa, which took just four days, and then there were four or five days at Tampa before the final sail to Cuba. Ships were to sail to their next destination in Santiago Harbor before they reunited on the Cuban coast. The ships passed Guantanamo Bay where the great war-ships had been sent off earlier and waiting off the coast. During landing offshore each man carried three days field rations and a hundred rounds of ammunition while the regiments had accumulated two rapid-fire Colt automatic guns and a dynamite gun. This is the story of the "Rough Riders" how they came to be picked, their character, and their journey abroad into unknown engagements of battle and for an unknown period of time.

After this traditional volunteer duty in the Spanish American War, Jordan Howard II returned not to Missouri but to Kentucky and the Kentucky River area where Daniel Boone had once settled Boonesborough. The marriages between Boone ancestors and the Arundell Howards would continue as Beverly Lewis Clark Goe, son of Benjamin Turner Goe, married Jordan Howard II's daughter, Josephine Howard. By tradition, Beverly Lewis Clark was a well-known politician in Washington, D. C. and made his travel back and forth from the states. On the Kentucky River they settled, prospered, and sought the rewards of knowing he had done his duty by faith for his country, family, and friends.

From colonial times to the present day, the Arundell Howards have done much to spread the Christian faith westward. Their duty to faith, country, family, and friends is evident in the many ranks they have held including in order Captain, Captain, Brigadier General, Militia Volunteer, Officer (unknown rank), and Militia Volunteer. The Arundell Howards were also the first Catholics to enter into Maryland, Kentucky, and Missouri. They helped spread the faith as did the church with men of faith including Reverend Benedict Joseph Flaget. Their part in the westward movement came by the settling in both Kentucky and Missouri with the early settlers in these states. Clement Howard, Sr. built a plantation west of Boonesborough where his son Philip Howard was born in 1812 in the county of Estill. Abraham Lincoln, a future President of the United States, would be born west of their plantation in Hardin County, Kentucky 1809. The coal production would increase dramatically around 1850 as would the building of railroads in Kentucky. The Louisville and Nashville railroad was developed to produce the tracks extending from Cincinnati to Tennessee. Philip Howard moved from one location to the next in the central area of the state from 1830 to 1850 where the main junction was located. He then moved westward to Dekalb County, Missouri sometime after 1850 where a main railroad hub was being built for the westward movement in Kansas City, Missouri. In 1859 a visit to St. Joseph, Missouri was made by Abraham Lincoln in conducting research for the railroad industry. The gateway to the west was now fully open and the transportation for further expansion needed to be developed.

There were many hardships during this time and in the region due to the Indian Wars from 1836 – 1890, Civil War, and gangsters. The Indian War was fought with the army, NCO's, and Indian scouts all with designated duties to repel attacks and safeguard routes. The Indian War would begin to diminish after the battle of Little Big Horn in June 25 –26, 1876 in Montana with the fall of General George Armstrong Custer. The Civil War would end in 1865 and soon after the assassination of Abraham Lincoln. The gangsters of note during this time were in the region of the mid-west and their main targets after 1870 were the railroads. During these trying times Jordan Wyatt Howard I died in the line of duty at the age of twenty five.

Upholding the values set forth by the Imperial College before and after dormancy by the Arundell Howards brought many hardships but not unnoticed by those who held to the same values. On March 23, 2007 full sanction was given for the Title of Count of the Holy Roman Empire by H.I. & R.H. Prinz Karl Friedrich von Deutschland, Herzog von Swabia, de jure

Charles VIII for the restored Holy Roman Empire making both Arundell, England and Arundell Howard, American nobility of Great Britain.

Judah was blessed and inherited the scepter due to the characteristics of unending strength, generous, sewer of seeds, humble, enduring, divine, prosperous, determined, and full of wisdom. Princes of the same characteristics would be builders of nations all from the same genealogical lineage with Judah as the father of the bloodline. Helenus had the characteristics of being divine as a seer for the Trojan royal family and rebuilt the city of Troy after the first war which would stand for six hundred years after his death. Clovis had the characteristics of endurance as he would win many battles while bringing Catholicism to the populace who were resistant to change. Charlemagne had the characteristics of being generous and determined and he sought to spread the faith and law to the populace under the Holy Roman Empire. Alfred the Great had the characteristics of being a sewer of seeds as he would create laws, print books of faith, promote education, and unify regions of England. Baron Thomas Arundell of Wardour had the characteristics of being a sewer of seeds and determination as he would defend the Holy Roman Empire in the east and increase it in the west.

The Holy Roman Empire has been the authority of the populace for much of European history due to the wisdom of the elected Emperor. All the characteristics of Judah stated have been inherent to those who reigned over the Temporal. Louis "The Pious" used his wisdom to hand down justice in a merciful manner during his turbulent reign. Rudolph II used his wisdom for unification against an invading army from the east and to reconcile the deteriorating religious position of the time. Francis II used his wisdom to become victorious over a rival to the Holy Roman Empire by showing the holder of the crown is elected and the holder of the scepter is inherited.

Judah in the Bible is said to be the lion, conqueror, and root of King David who made himself worthy for the coming of the Lord. His hand was always on the back of the enemy and thus the father's children shall adore him until the things come that are laid up for him.

The three precendances were adopted by the scepter holder to do the prevailing will of God. Judah accepted the scepter from Jacob to be the protectorate of the people during the holy war of Amun. For this he was highly recognized, promoting his will into a race of people known as the Trojan. His strength, abilities, and prosperity to the people brought him to a higher level with God and the Trojan, known as Zeus. Thus, the will of the people of the Troad became known as the worship to Zeus and his guidance through the priestess and the seers for over 2,000 years. The Trojans sought out justice through the guidance of Zeus during the three Trojan wars. Alexander the Great and the Greeks relied on the will of Zeus to bring justice to the people against the Persian Empire. Judah became more than a man of great respect, but a divine will in himself as they worshipped him as Zeus and carried on his traits and desire for justice. The adoption of this precedance allowed for both the Trojans and the Greeks to prosper and have wealth, while surviving attacks upon their citadel.

Christianity was accepted as the next precedance due to righteousness for the people, victories it gave to the scepter holder over rivals, and miracles brought forth by the spiritual such as St. Denis. This crucible of ideas spread fast and over a vast area, accepted by all who knew the burning desire to be prosperous, could only be obtained by this precedance. Thus, they were adopted by many over the centuries to win victories, Charlemagne, Alfred the Great, William Pincerna d' Alibini, and Edward I. Each of these men fought for the prosperity of the people, justice over invading armies, and the higher will of God spread forth by the spiritual.

In the beginning of the sixteenth century many battle fronts would open up in Europe, England, and America. The Thirty Years War, Ottoman War, Seven Years War, and Revolutionary War would be a test of will for righteousness, liberty, and religion. Duty and Faith would rise during these times as the next precedance. The Arundell Howard families found themselves at the center of these wars, but with great determination and the acceptance of this precedance they saw their way through colonial times and moved westward. A soldier with faith has been the directive since the time of both Clovis and Charlemagne. For as Hereward stated, a soldier blessed with the sword by a Christian soldier is also a soldier of God. Thus, the three precedances and the lineage of Judah's Scepter have been proven out, which another generation will be concurrent, while possibly adopting a new precedance to bring them closer to God.

Table Of Royal Titles

Adelaide de Vermandois	**Count**	
Adeliza	**Queen**	Dowager Queen of England who was married to Henry I and Countess of Arundell Castle from Louvania.
Aethelbert II	**King**	Region of Kent.
Aethelflaed		Lady of Mercia, daughter and heiress of Alfred the Great.
Alexander	**King** *Trojan*	The second Paris of Troy in the Third Trojan War.
Alfred The Great	**King**	The first King of England transforming the populace through Christianity and education, while defending it against the Danes.
Antenor I	**King** *Trojan*	Married Cambra, daughter of Belinus King of Britain.
Antenor II	**King** *Sicambri Trojan*	King of the Trojans under the refugees from Troy to Southeastern Europe.
Antenor IV	**King** *Frank*	
Antharius	**King**	Last King of the Sicambri Trojan aided by revolting Roman soldiers against Caesar. He died in battle with the Gauls.
Bartherus	**King** *Frank*	
Basabilano	**King** *Trojan*	
Basabiliano II	**King** *Trojan*	Last King of the Trojan of Troy before son Alexander undertakes third Trojan War.
Bassanus	*Sicambri Trojan*	Priest of Jupiter amongst the Sicambri Trojan and built the city of Bassanburg.
Bernard	**King** *Carolingian*	King of Italy and patriarch of the Papal State.

Charlemagne	**King Holy Roman Emperor** *Carolingian*	Holy Roman Emperor crowned by Pope Leo and King of the Franks. Created an empire throughout Europe.
Charles Martel	**Mayor of the Palace** *Carolingian*	Known as the "The Hammer" for is military victory against great odds in the Battle of Tours.
Childebert II	**King** *Merovingian*	
Childeric I	**King** *Merovingian*	
Clodius	**King** *Frank*	Father of Merowig starting the line of the Merovingians.
Clodius II	**King** *Frank*	
Clodius III	**King** *Frank*	
Clodomir III	**King** *Frank*	
Clodomir IV	**King** *Frank*	
Clothar I	**King** *Merovingian*	
Clovis	**King** *Merovingian*	King of all the Franks, adopting Christianity in all three-acceptance levels, founded Paris as the capital.
Dardanus	**King**	Son of Zarah (Zeus) and founder of Dardania.
Edmund Howard	**Lord**	Father of both Margaret, who married Thomas Arundell, and Katherine Howard, Queen of England.
Edward I	**King** *Plantagenet*	Plantagenet King of England who founded the House of Commons and the House of Lords while reconstructing the laws of the land.
Egbert	**King**	King of Wessex who won great victories throughout the lands after a stay in the kingdom of the Franks. He married a Frankish Princess names Redburga.
Egbert III	**King**	Region once known as Wessex. Married Redburh the possible daughter of Charlemagne. Grandfather of Alfred the Great.

Eliacor	**King** *Trojan*	
Esdron	**King** *Trojan*	
Ethelwulf	**King**	Region of Wessex. Father of Alfred the Great.
Farabert	**King** *Frank*	
Franco	**King** *Trojan*	Grandson of Helenus of Troy and great Trojan King.
Frankus	**King** *Trojan*	Battled the Romans with the Germans and Saxons and became the name used "Frank" by the peoples edict to represent them from what once was the Sicambri (Trojan).
Fulk III	**Count**	"The Black" of Anjou.
Fulk IV	**Count**	"Rechin" of Anjou.
Fulk V	**Count King of Jerusalem**	Married the daughter of Baldwin King of Jerusalem and Crusader to the Holy Land.
Gaberiano	**King** *Trojan*	
Gelio	**King** *Trojan*	
Genger	**King** *Trojan*	Son of Helenus and grandson of Priam King of Troy.
Geoffrey V	**Count Duke** *Plantagenet*	Ruler over Anjou, Maine, Normandy and England first in the line of the Plantagenets.
Godfrey II	**Count Duke**	
Herbert I	**Count** *Frank*	Regions of Vermandois, Senlis, Peronne and St. Quentin. Murdered by followers of Baldwin Lechauvelt of Flanders.
Helenus	**King** *Trojan*	A seer who was the son of Priam surviving the Trojan War and became lord of the lands of Greece and King of Troy.
Helenus II	**King** *Trojan*	
Henry II	**Count King** *Plantagenet*	First Plantagenet King of England and ruler over lands of Anjou, Maine, Normandy.
Henry III	**King** *Plantagenet*	
Herbert II	**Count** *Frank*	Regions of Vermandois and Troyes. Imprisoned Charles "The Simple" King of France at Peronne.

Hereward The Wake	**Knight**	Christian knight who won great fame in his campaign against the Normans under Duke William "the Conqueror".
Hilderic	**King** *Frank*	Built the castle Hildeburg on the Rhine and introduces culture and archaeology.
Ilus	**King**	Founder of Ilium that would later become the city of Troy.
Jacob (Kronos)		Traveled from the lands of Cannan and came upon an oracle from God in the form of a ladder filled with angels from heaven. Blessed his son Judah to be the builder of nations and having many princes from him.
John Howard	**Duke**	Second Duke of Norfolk who was commander of Richard III Plantagenet army during the battle of Bosworth Field.
John Lackland	**King** *Plantagenet*	Transferred title of King of England upon the death of his brother Richard "The Lionheart". Resolved the uprising of the Barons of England.
Judah (Jupiter)	**Zeus**	(Zheut – pater) "Father of the bloodline". Blessed by his father Jacob with the scepter for doing his will.
Katherine Howard	**Queen**	Married Henry VIII Tudor and reigned as Queen of England from 1540 – 1542.
Lambent II	**Count**	Region of Louvain.
Laomedon	**King** *Trojan*	
Leofric III	**Earl**	A nobleman in the region of Mercia who was the father of Hereward and had ties to the crown of England during King Harrods' reign.
Lothar I	**King Holy Roman Emperor** *Carolingian*	Co-Emperor with his father Louis "The Pious" whose struggle with his father and brothers for the crown would end divinely.
Louis I	**King Holy Roman Emperor** *Carolingian Frank*	Son of Charlemagne who sought to unite the kingdom of the Franks when it was split up after his father death.

Marcomir I	**King** *Sicambri Trojan*	King of the Sicambri Trojan who brought his people to the mouth of the Rhine to settle.
Marcomir III	**King** *Frank*	
Marcomir V	**King** *Frank*	
MarcomirIV	**King** *Frank*	Married Athilde, daughter of king of Britain.
Marcomir	**King** *Cimmerian Trojan*	
Merodochus	**King** *Sicambri Trojan*	Fought the Romans with the Cimbri but were defeated by Marius. Marched against the Gauls winning great victories.
Merowig	**King** *Merovingian Frank*	King of the Salian Franks who would begin the Merovigian Dynasty due to his victories in battle.
Nigel St. Sauvuer Neil II	**Baron**	Married Helena the daughter of Richard III of Normandy.
Nigel St. Sauvuer Neil III	**Viscount**	Present at the battle of Val-es-Dunes with Duke William of Normandy.
Odomir	**King** *Frank*	
Pepin	**Count** *Carolingian Frank*	Regions of Senlis, Peronne and St. Quentin.
Pepin I	**King** *Carolingian Frank*	Ruler over the lands of Italy, Lombardy Langobardians.
Pepin of Herstal	**Mayor of the Palace** *Frank*	He sought to dissolve Absolutism under Queen Brunhilda and the Merovingians.
Pharamond	**Duke** *Frank*	Fifth Duke of the Franks.
Plaserio	**King** *Trojan*	
Plaserio II	**King** *Trojan*	
Plbsron	**King** *Trojan*	
Plesron	**King** *Trojan*	

Priam	**King** *Trojan*	King of Troy saved during his childhood by his sister from the wrath of Hercules. King of Troy during the First Trojan War.
Priam II	**King** *Trojan*	
Richard de John de Cornwall	**King of the Romans**	Served in the crusades of Jerusalem and owned many lands in England including Cornwall. He became one of the wealthiest men in Europe and crowned by the Pope as King of the Romans.
Richemer	*Frank*	High Priest of the Franconians who fought with the Romans and Gauls.
Regnier I	**Count**	Region of Hainault.
Regnier II	**Count**	Region of Hainault.
Regnier III	**Count**	Region of Hainault.
Robert	**Count**	Regions of Troyes and Meaux.
Robert Howard	**Duke**	First Duke of Norfolk by marriage with Margaret Mowbray.
Sigebert I	**King** *Merovingian Frank*	King of the Franks whose wife Brunhilda would become the first Frankish Queen.
St. Arnulf	**Saint** *Arnulfian Frank*	
Theudebert II	**King** *Merovingian Frank*	Region of Austrasia.
Thomas Arundell Howard	**Count**	Son of Baron Thomas Arundell of Wardour, immigrated to America and established Howards Mount in Maryland.
Thomas Arundell	**Knight**	Knighted by Henry VII for his valor during the battle of Bosworth field.
Thomas Howard	**Duke**	Third Duke of Norfolk who was imprisoned by Henry VII for aiding Richard III in the Battle of Bosworth Field.
Thomas Arundell of Wardour	**Baron Count**	Soldier of Fortune in valor for Rudolph II, Holy Roman Emperor, and a zealous Catholic within the court of Elizabeth I and James I.

Thomas Mowbray	**Duke**	Title in the region of Norfolk that would pass to the Howards by the marriage of his daughter Margaret.
Tros	**King**	Founder of Troy beginning the Trojan lineage.
William Pincerna d' Albini I	**Earl**	Present during the battle of Val-es-Dunes and accompanied Duke William of Normandy in the battle of Hastings. Settled the dispute between Henry I and Stephen for the Crown of England.
William d' Albini II	**Earl**	Owner of Arundell Castle.
William d' Albini III	**Earl**	Owner of Arundell Castle which was at one time taken by John Lackland and then granted back upon payment to the Crown.
Wihtred Oiscinga	**King**	Region of Kent.
Zarah	**Zeus**	(Zheut – pater) "Father of the bloodline". Scepter holder to the lineage of the Trojans. Married Electra Roma one of seven Pleiades.

ZEUS
WIVES, CONSORTS, CHILDREN

Wives Consorts	Children			
Ananke	Moirae			
Demeter	Persephone			
Dione	Aphrodite			
Hera	Ares	Eiliethyia	Hephaestus	Hebe
Eos	Ersa			
Eris	Limos			
Leto	Apollo	Artemis		
Maia	Hermes			
Metis	Athena			
Mnemosyne	Muses			
Selene	Ersa	Nemean Lion	Pandia	
Thalassa Aphrodite				
Themis	Astraea	Nemesis	Horae	Moirae
Aegina	Aeacus			
Alcmene	Heracles (Hercules)			
Antiope	Amphion	Zethus		
Callisto	Arcas			
Carme	Britomartis			
Danae	Perseus			
Elara	Tityas			
Electra Roma	Dardanus	Iasion		
Europa	Minos	Rhadamanthys	Sarpedon	
Eurynome	Aglaea	Euphrosyne	Thalia	

Himalia	Kronios	Spartaios	Kytos
Iodame	Thebe		
Io	Epaphus		
Lamia			
Laodamia	Sarpedon		
Leda	Polydeuces	Helen	
Maera	Locrus		
Niobe	Argos	Pelasgus	
Olympias	Alexander the Great		
Plouto	Tantalus		
Podarge	Balius	Xanthus	
Pyrrha	Hellen		
Semele	Dionysus		
Taygete	Lacedaemon		
Thalia	Palici		

Genealogy of Troy

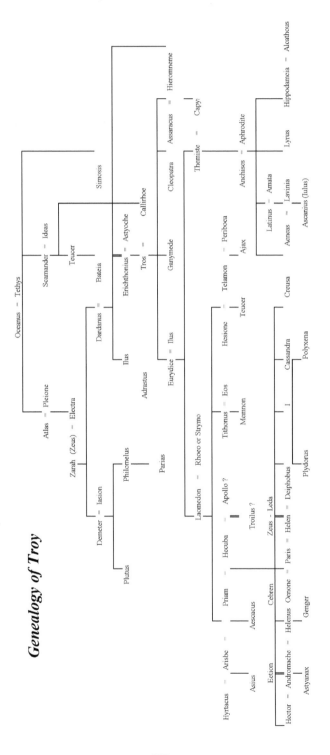

Genealogy of Merovingian Dynasty

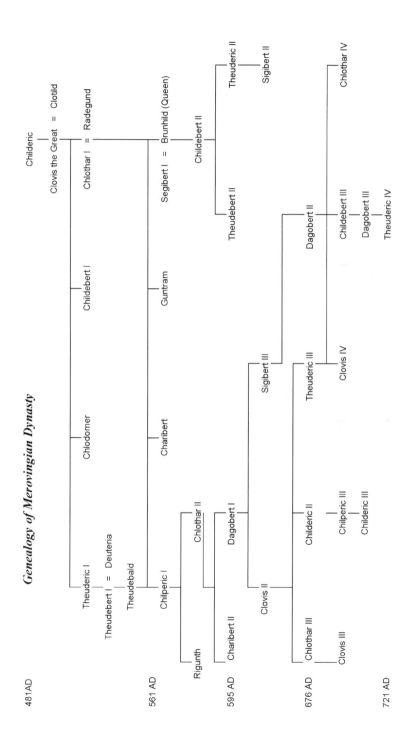

Genealogy of Carolingian Dynasty

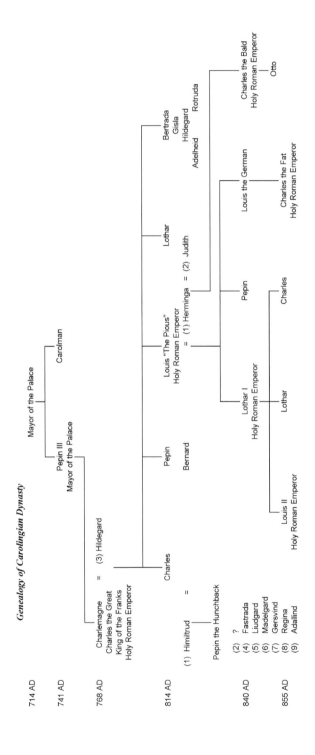

714 AD

741 AD

768 AD

814 AD

840 AD

855 AD

Mayor of the Palace

Pepin III
Mayor of the Palace

Carolman

Charlemagne   =   (3) Hildegard
Charles the Great
King of the Franks
Holy Roman Emperor

Charles

(1) Himiltrud   =

Pepin the Hunchback

(2) ?
(4) Fastrada
(5) Liudgard
(6) Madelgard
(7) Gersvind
(8) Regina
(9) Adalind

Pepin

Bernard

Louis "The Pious"
Holy Roman Emperor
= (1) Herminga = (2) Judith

Lothar

Lothar I
Holy Roman Emperor

Louis II
Holy Roman Emperor

Pepin

Lothar

Charles

Bertrada
Gisla
Hildegard
Adelheid   Rotruda

Louis the German

Charles the Fat
Holy Roman Emperor

Charles the Bald
Holy Roman Emperor

Otto

154

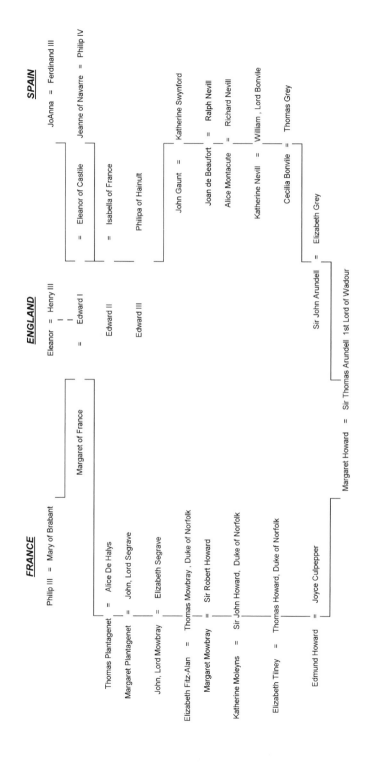

FRANCE

Philip III = Mary of Brabant

ENGLAND

Eleanor = Henry III

SPAIN

JoAnna = Ferdinand III

= Edward I = Eleanor of Castile

Jeanne of Navarre = Philip IV

Edward II = Isabella of France

Edward III

Philipa of Hainult

Margaret of France

John Gaunt = Katherine Swynford

Joan de Beaufort = Ralph Nevill

Alice Montacute = Richard Nevill

Katherine Nevill = William , Lord Bonvile

Cecilia Bonvile = Thomas Grey

Thomas Plantagenet = Alice De Halys

Margaret Plantagenet = John, Lord Segrave

John, Lord Mowbray = Elizabeth Segrave

Elizabeth Fitz-Alan = Thomas Mowbray , Duke of Norfolk

Margaret Mowbray = Sir Robert Howard

Katherine Moleyns = Sir John Howard, Duke of Norfolk

Elizabeth Tilney = Thomas Howard, Duke of Norfolk

Edmund Howard = Joyce Culpepper

Sir John Arundell = Elizabeth Grey

Margaret Howard = Sir Thomas Arundell 1st Lord of Wadour

Notes

Preface

1. *Our wills, therefore, exist*: "City of God" translated by Marcus Dods, D.D. 1994, Modern Library Edition Random House Inc., N.Y., pg. 157 [Book V, Section 10]
2. *For it is to God:* Ibid. pg. 278 [Book VIII, Section 27]
3. *This is the origin :* Ibid. pg. 693 [Book XIX, Section 14]

I

4. *See, he says. the smell:* "The Holy Bible Containing the Old and New Testaments" translated out of the original tongues 1870, American Bible Society, N.Y., pg.27 [Gen. C 27, L 27-29, L 33]
5. *And he came to a place:* Ibid. pg. 28 [Gen. C 28, L 10-19]
6. *It said to be oblong :* "Judahs' Scepter and Joseph's Birthright" by Rev. J. H. Allen 1922, A. A. Beauchamp, Boston, MA pg. 252
7. *The regal chair holding* : Ibid pg. 252
8. *Jacob Journey to Egypt :* "The New Schaff-Herzog Encyclopedia of Religious Knowledge" 1977, Vol. VI, pg. 74
9. *The latter was also :* "The Mystery of the Oracles" by Philip Vandenberg 1982, MacMillan Publishing Co. Inc., N.Y. pg. 59
10. *Judah, thy brethren thy :* "The Holy Bible Containing the Old and New Testaments" translated out of the original tongues 1870, American Bible Society, N.Y., pg. 50 [Gen. C 49, L 8-12]
11. *Judah is declared to :* "Symbols of Our Celto-Saxon Heritage" by W. H. Bennett 1976, Covenant Books, London pg. 25
12. *Thus, the scepter is* : "Judahs' Scepter and Joseph's Birthright" by Rev. J. H. Allen 1922, A. A. Beauchamp, Boston, MA pg. 36
13. *The heritage given down* : Ibid pg.37
14. *The promise given would* : Ibid pg. 150
15. *The story of Zarah is* : Ibid pg.204

16. *The tribe of Zarah* : "Symbols of Our Celto-Saxon Heritage" by W. H. Bennett 1976, Covenant Books, London pg. 113

17. *The biblical sons of* : "Judah's Scepter and Joseph's Birthright" by Rev. J. H. Allen 1922, A. A. Beauchamp, Boston, MA pg. 204

18. *The writings of Sanchuniathon's* : "The New Schaff-Herzog Encyclopedia of Religious Knowledge" 1977, Vol. X, pg. 197 –199

19. *In the Aeneid by* : "The Aeneid of Virgil by Virgil" translated by William Morris 1900, Longmans, Green and Co, Book III

20. *This is the Phoenician* : "Philo of Byblos the Phoenician History" by Harold W. Attridge and Robert A. Oden, Jr. 1981, The Catholic Biblical Association of America, Washington D.C. , pg. 61

21. *He is portrayed by* : "The Two Babylons" by the Rev. Alexander Hislop 1959, Loizeaux Brothers Inc. New Jersey, pg. 295

22. *Titans were considered adversary* : Ibid pg. 295

23. *Electra was known as* : "Ilios: The City and Country of the Trojans" by Heinrich Schliemann 1880, Haper, N.Y., pg. 152

24. *Hear me, said he* : "Iliad by Homer" translated by Samuel Butler 1898, Longsman, Green and Co., Book I

25. *All had then been lost* : Ibid Book I

26. *But the son of Peleus* : Ibid Book I

27. *I shall have trouble* : Ibid Book VIII

28. *The origins of the oracle* : "Herodotus" Rev. William Beloe 1830, Jones & Co., London, pg. 87

29. *It is from here* : "The Mystery of the Oracles" by Philip Vandenberg 1982, MacMillan Publishing Co. Inc., N.Y., pg. 164

30. *The names for the gods* : "Herodotus" Rev. William Beloe 1830, Jones & Co., London, pg. 87

31. *One day while shepherding* : "Hesiod, the Homeric Hymns, and Homerica by Homer" translated by Evelyn-White, Hugh Gerard 1924, Life of Hesiod

32. *Muses of Pieria who* : Ibid Work Days 1-10

33. *The two things Hesiod* : Ibid Work Days 293-319

34. *The characteristics he possessed* : "The Will of Zeus" by Strongfellow Barr 1961, Lippincott, PA, pg. 440

35. *Alexander founded the first* : Ibid pg. 404

36. *The Great Macedonian King* : "Ilios: The City and Country of the Trojans" by Heinrich Schliemann 1880, Harper, Bronx, N.Y., pg. 171

37. *The will of Zeus* : "The Mystery of the Oracles" by Philipp Vandenberg 1982, MacMillan Publishing Co. Inc., N.Y. pg. 246-247

38. *Dardanus had a son* : "Ilios: The City and Country of the Trojans" by Heinrich Schliemann 1880, Harper, N.Y., pg. 119, 152

39. *Dardanus was a son* : "Compendium of World History" Vol. 2, by Herman L. Hoeh 1963, 1966, 1969 Edition pg. 81, 88

40. *Dardanus and his people* : "Symbols of Our Celto-Saxon Heritage" by W. H. Bennett 1976, Covenant Books, London pg. 119

41. *However, a story had Dardanus* : "The Aeneid of Virgil by Virgil" translated by William Morris 1900, Longmans, Greene and Co., Book III

42. *The Egyptians, Hittites, Amazons* : "Ilios: The City and Country of the Trojans" by Heinrich Schliemann 1880, Harper, N. Y., pg. 122-123

43. *The Hittite Empire was*: Ibid pg. 159

44. *The Dominions of the Troad* : Ibid pg. 132

45. *The Trojans and their names* : Ibid pg. 120

46. *The founder of Troy* : Ibid pg. 153, 643

47. *The memory of the correct :* "Troy and its Remains" by Dr. Henry Schliemann 1875, John Murray , Albemarle Street, London, pg. 43

48. *It wasn't until 1870* : Ibid pg. 343

49. *The treasures found might* : Ibid pg. 17-20

50. *Dorpfelds' discoveries, however, seemed* : "Schliemann's Excavations" by Karl Schuchardt and Eugenie Strong 1891, MacMillan and Co., London, pg. 325-327

51. *The size of the city* : "Ilios: The City and Country of the Trojans" by Heinrich Schliemann 1880, Harper, N.Y., vii

52. *Troy was built of* : Ibid pg. 140

53. *The city of Troy* : Ibid pg. 139

54. *Blegen, Evans, and Ventris* : "The Decipherment of Linear B" John Chadwick 2003, Cambridge University Press, pg. 36-.37

55. *It was found through* : Ibid pg. 102-104

56. *Neoptolemus captured Helenus when* : "The Aeneid of Virgil by Virgil" translated by William Morris 1900, Longmans, Greene and Co., Book III

57. *Helenus in the story:* "Iliad by Homer translated by Samuel Butler 1898, Longmans, Green and Co., Book VI

58. *He held his ground* : Ibid Book XIII

59. *Helenus was the founder* : "The Aeneid of Virgil by Virgil" translated by William Morris 1900, Longmans, Greene and Co., Book III

60. *Aeneas decides to make* : Ibid Book II

61. *Aeneas was implored to* : Ibid Book II

62. *When Aeneas ship was* : Ibid Book III

63. *The Trojan royal family* : "Compendium of World History" Vol. 2, by Herman L. Hoeh 1963, 1966, 1969 Edition pg. 131

64. *The Spanish historian Bartholome Gutierrez* : "Historia Del Estado Presente Y Antiguo, De La Mui Noble Y Mui Leal Ciudad De Xerez De La Frontera" by Bartholome Gutierrez 1886, pg. 165-168

65. *Alexander (Paris) was the* : "Compendium of World History" Vol. 2, by Herman L. Hoeh 1963, 1966, 1969 Edition pg. 132-133

66. *The area settled was* : Ibid pg. 134-139

67. *Judah they brethren shall* : "The Holy Bible Containing the Old and New Testaments" translated out of the original tongues 1870, American Bible Society, N.Y., pg. 50 [Gen. C 49, L 8-12]

III

68. *The Franks would begin* : "The Franks From Their First Appearance in History to the Death of King Pepin" by Walter C. Perry 1857, Longman, Brown, Green, Longmans, and Roberts, pg. 353-356

69. *The brother line of the* : "Judah's Scepter and Joseph's Birthright" by Rev. J. H. Allen 1922, A. A. Beauchamp, Boston, MA pg. 215

70. *Generals that battled with* : "The Franks From Their First Appearance in History to the Death of King Pepin" by Walter C. Perry 1857, Longman, Brown, Green, Longmans, and Roberts, pg. 57-64

71. *Julianretook Cologneand* : "The Franks" Lewis Sergeant 1898, G. P. Putnam's Sons, N.Y., pg. 88-91

72. *Merowig and his son* : Ibid pg. 82

73. *Facts about Childeric I are* : "The Franksby Edward James 1988, Basil Blackwell Inc. N.Y., pg. 61

74. *Clovis found it necessary:* "The Franks From Their First Appearance in History to the Death of King Pepin" by Walter C. Perry 1857, Longman, Brown, Green, Longmans, and Roberts, pg. 371-373

75. *Victories came quickly to:* Ibid pg. 76-77

76. *Burgundyleader was Gundobad:* Ibid pg. 82-82

77. *The Catholic Church supported* : "The Franks" Lewis Sergeant 1898, G. P. Putnam's Sons, N.Y., pg. 111-113

78. *A great change had* : "The Mystery of the Oracles" by Philipp Vandenberg 1982, MacMillan Publishing Co. Inc., N.Y. pg. 271-272

79. *The Frankstook over* : "The Franks From Their First Appearance in History to the Death of King Pepin" by Walter C. Perry 1857, Longman, Brown, Green, Longmans, and Roberts, pg. 84-89

80. *In 511 Clovis died* : "The Franks" Lewis Sergeant 1898, G. P. Putnam's Sons, N.Y., pg. 152

81. *An example of this is* : "Tales of the Early Franksby Augustin Thierry and translated by M.F.O. Jenkins 1977, University of Alabama Press, pg. 10

82. *The kingdom would be* : "The Franks From Their First Appearance in History to the Death of King Pepin" by Walter C. Perry 1857, Longman, Brown, Green, Longmans, and Roberts, pg. 128

83. *The death of Charibert*: "The Franks" Lewis Sergeant 1898, G. P. Putnam's Sons, N.Y., pg. 182

84. *Chilperic sought to engage* : "The History of Franceby Parke Godwin 1860, Haper and Brothers, N.Y. pg. 319-321

85. *There was now for* : Ibid 322-323

86. *An estimate around 13* : "The Franksby Edward James 1988, Basil Blackwell Inc. N.Y., pg. 150-151

87. *The official in charge* : "The Franks From Their First Appearance in History to the Death of King Pepin" by Walter C. Perry 1857, Longman, Brown, Green, Longmans, and Roberts, pg. 474-476, 427-429

IV

88. *These assemblies would be* : "The History of France" by Parke Godwin 1860, Haper and Brothers, N.Y. pg. 227-228

89. *Pepinthe Younger of Austrasian* : Ibid pg. 92-108

90. *The Moslem army had* : Ibid pg. 105-106

91. *Charles Martel and his son* : Ibid pg. 107-108

92. *The great legend would* : "The Franks From Their First Appearance in History to the Death of King Pepin" by Walter C. Perry 1857, Longman, Brown, Green, Longmans, and Roberts, pg. 318-320

93. *Pope Hadrian baptized him* : "Carolingian Chronicles Royal Frankish Annals and Nithard's Histories" by Bernard Walter Scholz 1970, The University of Michigan Press, pg. 59

94. *Accounts are made in* : Ibid pg. 59, 81, 89

95. *His works portray Charlemagne* : "The Life of Charlemagne" by Einhard translated by Samuel Epes Turner 1880, Harper and Brother, pg. 30

96. *The education of the royal* : Ibid pg. 51, 61-62

97. *This was not the* : Ibid pg. 60
98. *He would later take*: Ibid pg. 12
99. *His first test in* : Ibid pg. 22, 23
100. *The two examples of* : Ibid pg. 29
101. *One of the most bloody* : Ibid pg. 37
102. *Frankish army used during*: "Daily Life in the World of Charlemagne" by Jo Ann McNamara 1978, University of Pennsylvania Press, pg. 77
103. *Within this is the Frankish* : Ibid pg. 4,6
104. *On Christmas Day 801 AD* : "Carolingian Chronicles Royal Frankish Annals and Nithard's Histories" by Bernard Walter Scholz 1970, The University of Michigan Press, pg. 81
105. *Charles the Great son* : "Charlemagne" by Rev. Edward L. Cutts 1882, E & J.B. Young and Co., N.Y., pg. 282-283
106. *The palace at Aachen* : "Daily Life in the World of Charlemagne" by Jo Ann McNamara 1978, University of Pennsylvania Press, pg. 42-43
107. *It was to resemble :* "The Horizon Book of Great Cathedrals" by The Editors of Horizon Magazine 1984, Bonanza Books, American Heritage Publishing Co. Inc., N.Y. pg. 212
108. *Besides Aachen the preferred*: "Daily Life in the World of Charlemagne" by Jo Ann McNamara 1978, University of Pennsylvania Press, pg. 41
109. *After pursuit did not* : "Charlemagne: Father of a Continent" by Alessandro Barbero 2004, University of California Press, 47-48
110. *The Eastern Germans would* : "Charlemagne" by Roger Collins 1998, University of Toronto Press Inc., Toronto, pg. 150-151
111. *Charlemagne upheld this as* : "The Life of Charlemagne" by Einhard translated by Samuel Epes Turner 1880, Harper and Brother, pg. 64
112. *Many gifts were given* : Ibid pg. 43-44
113. *The Byzantine Empire succeeded* : "The Holy Roman Empire" by James Bryce 1920, MacMillan and Co. Ltd., St. Martin's Street, London, pg. 64
114. *The divine framework of* : Ibid pg. 104
115. *Pepin, the son of Charlemagne* : "Carolingian Chronicles Royal Frankish Annals and Nithard's Histories" by Bernard Walter Scholz 1970, The University of Michigan Press, pg. 89
116. *Bernard grandson of Charlemagne* : Ibid pg. 95
117. *Louis put all the above* : Ibid pg. 130
118. *Another struggle would begin* : Ibid pg. 168

V

119. *The House of Anjou* : "Fulk Nerra: the Neo-Roman Consul" by Bernard S. Bachrach 1993, University of California Press, Berkley, pg. 4

120. *Fulk Nerra was the* : Ibid pg. 27-28

121. *He was a Christian* : "The Plantagenet Chronicles" by Elizabeth Hallam 1986, Weidenfeld and Nicolson N.Y., pg. 25

122. *The black monks of* : Ibid pg. 29

123. *Baldwin II was the defender* : "Henry II" by W. L. Warren 1973, University of California Press, Berkeley and Los Angeles, CA pg.605

124. *The Byzantine Empire was* : "The Shaping of France" by Isaac Asimov 1972, Houghton Mifflin Co. Boston, pg. 28-30

125. *Roland was one of* : "Charlemagne" by Rev. Edward L. Cutts 1882, E. & J. B. Young and Co., N. Y., pg. 257-259

126. *Geoffrey first conquest would* : "The Plantagenet Chronicles" by Elizabeth Hallam 1986, Weidenfeld and Nicolson N.Y., pg. 62

127. *In 1153 Henry II landed* : "The Plantagenet Chronicles" by Elizabeth Hallam 1986, Weidenfeld and Nicolson N.Y., [part 1 heading], pg. 88

128. *Henry II Plantagenet was now* : "Court, Household, and Itinerary of Henry II" by Rev. R.W. Eyton M.A. 1878, Taylor and Co., London, pg. x, xi

129. *Henry II Plantagenet brought* : "Castles and Fortresses" by Robin S. Oggins1995, Michael Friedman Publishing Group Inc. pg. 23, 56.58-59

130. *Policies used to reconstruct* : "Henry II" by W. L. Warren 1973, University of California Press, Berkeley and Los Angeles, CA, pg. 208-210

131. *When Richard was of* : "A History of the Life of Richard Coeur-De-Lion" by G. P. R. James Esq. 1842, Saunders and Otley, London, pg. 318

132. *To defend his lands* : "The Shaping of France" by Isaac Asimov 1972, Houghton Mifflin Co. Boston, pg. 68

133. *Castles would also become* : "Castles and Fortresses" by Robin S. Oggins1995, Michael Friedman Publishing Group Inc. pg. 91

134. *Richard the Lionheart* : "A History of the Life of Richard Coeur-De-Lion" by G. P. R. James Esq. 1842, Saunders and Otley, London, pg. 5

135. *In 1177 Henry II and* : Ibid pg. 238-240

136. *In Tours 1187 after* : "Henry II" by W. L. Warren 1973, University of California Press, Berkeley and Los Angeles, CA pg. 607

137. *Another turn of events* : "John Lackland" by Kate Norgate 1902, MacMillan and Co. Ltd., New York, pg. 26-29

138. *The first crusade in* : "A History of the Crusades" Steven Runciman 1951, Cambridge University Press, United Kingdom, pg. 116-117

139. *The first step of* : "The Crusades and the Crusaders" by John George Edgar 1860, Ticknor and Fields, Boston, pg. 173-175

140. *The next step was* : Ibid pg. 179

141. *The ships arrived as* : Ibid pg. 184-188

142. *Richard then headed south* : Ibid pg. 198-200

143. *Edward I King of England* : "The Three Edward's" by Thomas B. Costain 1958, Doubleday and Co. Inc. N.Y. pg. 16-17

144. *Edward I was crowned* : Ibid pg. 21

145. *Windsor Castle was the* : Ibid pg. 27

146. *There were later castles* : "Castles and Fortresses" by Robin S. Oggins1995, Michael Friedman Publishing Group Inc. pg. 15, 19-20, 46, 47

147. *Edward I maintained a* : "The Three Edward's" by Thomas B. Costain 1958, Doubleday and Co. Inc. N.Y. pg. 47-48

148. *A final issue that* : Ibid pg. 88

149. *A time of turmoil came* : "Bosworth Field" by A.L. Rowse 1966, Doubleday and Co., Inc., Garden City, N.Y., pg. 6

150. *A clash between the* : Ibid pg. 2

151. *This would begin the* : "The Last Plantagenets" by Thomas B. Costain 1962, Doubleday and Co. Inc., Garden City, N.Y. , pg. 1

152. *In this struggle between* : "Bosworth Field" by A.L. Rowse 1966, Doubleday and Co., Inc., Garden City, N.Y., pg. 136

VI

153. *Upon Egbert return he* : "Kings and Kingdoms of Early Anglo-Saxon England" by Barbara Yorke 1990, B.A. Seaby Ltd., pg. 32, 148

154. *In 871 King Alfred* : "King Alfred of England" by Jacob Abbott 1849, Harper & Brothers, Chpt. VII Reverses

155. *Alfred the Great had* : Ibid Chpt. IV Alfred's Early Years

156. *The marriage was to* : Ibid Chpt. VI Alfred's Accession to the Throne

157. *Long ships built to* : Ibid Chpt. XII The Close of Life

158. *In youth he was* : Ibid Chpt. XI Character of Alfred's Reign

159. *Alfred would read books* : "The Whole Works of King Alfred the Great" by Messrs. J.F. Smith and Co., Oxford and Cambridge 1852, pg. 15
160. *The excerpts here show* : Ibid pg. 134
161. *The one item that* : "Hereward" by Victor Head 1995, Allan Sutton Publishing, pg. 26
162. *Hereward is shown to* : Ibid pg. 122, Appendix B
163. *Hereward was the son* : "Hereward, The Last of the English" by Charles Kingsley 1891, Macmillan and Company, London and New York, pg. 9-11
164. *Torfrida was a noble* : Ibid pg. 46-47
165. *Then there is Godfrey II* : "Henry II" by W. L. Warren 1973, University of California Press, Berkeley and Los Angeles, CA pg. 606
166. *The Battle of Hastings* : "Hereward, The Last of the English" by Charles Kingsley 1891, Macmillan and Company, London and New York, pg. 83-84
167. *Hereward in short time* : Ibid pg. 86-89
168. *The knights seized all* : Ibid pg. 118
169. *Thousands were killed within* : Ibid pg. 165-166
170. *Robert (Hereward) Howard of* : "The Early Genealogical History of the House of Arundell" by John Pym Yeatman 1882, Mitchell and Hughes, London, pg. 342
171. *William Howard was the* : Ibid pg. 343
172. *The second grand marriage* : "The Thomas Book: Sir Rhys ap Thomas K.G." by Lawrence Buckley Thomas 1896, Henry T. Thomas Co., pg. 366
173. *More significant in his* : "The Ebbs and Flows of Fortune: The Life of Thomas Howard Third Duke of Norfolk" by David M. Head 1995, University of Georgia Press, Georgia, pg. 12-22
174. *Thomas Howard Earl of Arundell* : "The Life, Correspondence & Collections of Thomas Howard, Earl of Arundell" by Mary Frederica Sophia Hervey 1921, University Press, Cambridge, pg. 66-67
175. *A return visit was* : Ibid pg. 63
176. *In 1621 he began* : Ibid pg. 272-273
177. *The future Queen's grandmother* : "The Six Wives of Herny VIII" by Alison Weir 1991, Grove Press, N. Y., pg. 416, 431, 435
178. *As Yeatman has documented* : "The Early Genealogical History of the House of Arundell" by John Pym Yeatman 1882, Mitchell and Hughes, London, pg. 344
179. *The Duke of Norfolk* : Ibid pg. 345

VII

180. *Adeliza was an elegant* : "The Three Edward's" by Thomas B. Costain 1958, Doubleday and Co. Inc. N.Y. pg. 260-261

181. *Her stay in the royal* : "The Early Genealogical History of the House of Arundell" by John Pym Yeatman 1882, Mitchell and Hughes, London, pg. 285

182. *The Dukes of Normandy* : "The Norman's and the Norman Conquest" by R. Allen Brown 1834, Thomas Y. Crowell Co. Inc., N.Y., pg. 20-23

183. *Dukes of Normandy were* : Ibid pg. 27-46

184. *Their system of governing* : Ibid pg.. 224

185. *In 1047 William gained* : Ibid pg. 56-58

186. *The Norman invasion of* : Ibid pg. 214

187. *Nigel St. Sauvuer (Neil III)* : "A History of Wales: From Earliest Times to the Edwardian Conquest" by Sir John Edward Lloyd, M. A., D. Litt., F.B.A 1967, Longmans, Green and Co. Ltd., London, Vol. I, II pg.382

188. *In 1077 he fought* : "Journal of the Architectural, Archaeological, and Historical Society, for the County, City and Neighborhood of Chester", Vol. II. from December 1855 to 1862, Printed at the Courant Office, Chester pg. 3

189. *This was the seat* : Ibid pg. 15

190. *The motte-and-bailey* : "The Norman's and the Norman Conquest" by R. Allen Brown 1834, Thomas Y. Crowell Co. Inc., N.Y., pg. 44

191. *The name has many* : "The Early Genealogical History of the House of Arundell" by John Pym Yeatman 1882, Mitchell and Hughes, London, pg. 71

192. *There was only one* : Ibid pg. 103-109

193. *One matter was an* : Ibid pg. 7

194. *William d" Albini, Earl of Chichester* : Ibid pg. 287

195. *The builders of Arundell* : Ibid pg. 1-3

196. *There are four great* : Ibid pg. 69-70

197. *The meaning of Earl* : Ibid pg. 3-5

198. *A story of one* : Ibid pg. 222

199. *John Arundell I inherited* : Ibid pg. 252-255

200. *A grant to her grandfather* : Ibid pg. 257-260

201. *The prosperity of the* : Ibid pg. 261

202. *The marriage gave him* : Ibid pg. 267-273

203. *At some time during* : Ibid pg. 270

VIII

204. *A letter was written* : "The Early Genealogical History of the House of Arundell" by John Pym Yeatman 1882, Mitchell and Hughes, London, pg. 275

205. *It is said he immediately* : Ibid pg. 254

206. *The Habsburg's were a* : "A History of the Habsburg Empire 1526 – 1918" by Robert A. Kann 1977, University California Press Ltd., Berkley, Los Angeles, London pg. 2-5

207. *The descendants of the* : Ibid pg. 7

208. *Emperor Rudolph II was in* : "The Holy Roman Empire" by James Bryce 1920, MacMillan and Co. Ltd., St. Martin's Street, London, pg. 380-384

209. *These are the three* : Ibid pg. 25

210. *Two struggles by the* : "A History of the Habsburg Empire 1526 – 1918" by Robert A. Kann 1977, University California Press Ltd., Berkley, Los Angeles, London pg. 36-41

211. *The Ottoman Empire was* : "The Ottoman Centuries: The Rise and Fall of the Turkish Empire" by Lord Kinross 1977, William Morrow and Co. Inc., N. Y. pg. 27-34

212. *Baron Thomas Arundell of* : "The Early Genealogical History of the House of Arundell" by John Pym Yeatman 1882, Mitchell and Hughes, London, pg. 275-277

213. *Rudolph II, by the favor* : Ibid pg. 275

214. *Recognition by Elizabeth I would* : Ibid pg. 277

215. *The breakdowns from civilians* : "England in America 1580-1652" by Lyon Gardiner Tyler 1904, Harper and Brothers

216. *A voyage to New England* : Ibid

217. *In 1633 the second Lord* : Ibid

218. *Thomas Arundell Howard the* : St. Mary's County Historical Society, Mernards Map

219. *The Colony was set* : "Side-Lights on Maryland History" by Hester Dorsey Richardson 1913, Williams and Wilkins Co., Baltimore, pg. 65-71, 257

220. *Due to religious issues* : Ibid pg. 237

221. *The descendants would carry* : "Durbin-Witt-Wagers, Richardson-Stephens, and related families via Maryland, Virginia, Kentucky", Missouri by Pearl Mix Cox 1907, Pub. By Pearl M. Cox, Missouri pg. 526

222. *Rev. H. B. Schulte of St. Mark's* : "History of Kentucky" by William Elsey Connelly and E. M. Coulter 1922, The American Historical Society, Chicago and N.Y., pg. 255

223. *narrated by Rev. H. B. Schulte* : "The Register of the Kentucky Historical Society" by Kentucky Historical Society 1911, Frankfurt, KY pg. 95

224. *In 1753 and emissary* : "Crucible of War: The Seven Years' War and the Fate of Empire in British North America 1754 – 1766" by Fred Anderson 2000, Alfred A. Knopf N.Y. pg. 41

225. *On the European front* : Ibid pg. 126-129

226. *The condition of the Seven* : "History of Maryland from its First Settlement in 1634 to the Year 1848" by James McSherry 1849, John Murphy, Baltimore, MD, pg. 100-103, 127-146

227. *He served under many* : "The Life of Daniel Boone" by Lyman C. Draper LL.D. , edited by Ted Franklin Belue 1998, Stackpole Books, PA, pg. 128-138

228. *Secondly the Governor of* : "Side-Lights on Maryland History" by Hester Dorsey Richardson 1913, Williams and Wilkins Co., Baltimore, pg. 361-365

229. *British officers such as* : "History of Maryland from its First Settlement in 1634 to the Year 1848" by James McSherry 1849, John Murphy, Baltimore, MD, pg. 136-137

230. *In 1774 a new* : "Daniel Boone: The Life and Legend of an American Pioneer" by John Mack Faragher 1992, Henry Holt and Company, N.Y., pg. 99-105

231. *Despite attacks from the* : "The Life of Daniel Boone" by Lyman C. Draper LL.D. , edited by Ted Franklin Belue 1998, Stackpole Books, PA pg. 440

232. *He would also join* : Ibid pg. 453-454

233. *Clement was the first of* : "The Centenary of Catholicity in Kentucky" by Hon. Ben J. Webb 1884, Charles A Rogers pg. 26-27, 92

234. *In 1799 Daniel Boone* : "The Life of Daniel Boone" by Lyman C. Draper LL.D. , edited by Ted Franklin Belue 1998, Stackpole Books, PA pg. 533

235. *The sign up places* : "The Rough Riders" by Theodore Roosevelt 1899, section I Raising the Regiment

236. *However, because the number* : Ibid section I

237. *Allyn Capron was one* : Ibid section I

238. *Ships were to sail* : Ibid section section II To Cuba

Secondary Sources

"Egypt Place in Universal History: An Historical Investigation in Five Books" Vol. II, by Christian C. J. Bunsen, D. Ph & D. C. L., translated from the German by Charles H. Cottrell, Esq. M. A., 1854, Longman, Brown and Green, and Longmans, London

"The Wars in Syria and Palestine of Thutmose III" by Donald B. Redford 2003, Koninklijke Brill NV, Leiden, The Netherlands

"The Oracle: The Lost Secrets and Hidden Messages of Ancient Delphi" by William J. Broad 2006, The Penguin Press

"Henry I King of England and Duke of Normandy" by Judith A. Green 2006, Cambridge University Press, N. Y.

"King Arthur in Legend and History" Ed. by Richard White 1998, Routledge, N.Y.

"The Founding Fathers George Washington a Biography in His Own Words" Ed. by Ralph K. Andrist 1972, Newsweek, N.Y., Harper & Row, Publishers Inc.

"The Spanish War and American Epic – 1898" by G. J. A. O'Toole 1984, W. W. Norton & Company, N.Y.

"The 1600's Headlines in History" by Louise I. Gerdes 2001, Greenhaven Press Inc.

St. Mary's Maryland Historical Society

INDEX